Library of
Davidson College

THESEUS AS SON AND STEPSON

THESEUS AS SON AND STEPSON

A tentative illustration of Greek mythological mentality

by

CHRISTIANE SOURVINOU-INWOOD

University of London
INSTITUTE OF CLASSICAL STUDIES

Bulletin Supplement No. 40

1979

Published and distributed by
Institute of Classical Studies
31 – 34 Gordon Square, London WC1H OPY

SBN 900587 39 3

Contents

Acknowledgments	vii
List of Illustrations	ix
1. Preface	1
2. Was Theseus a matricide manqué?	3
3. Excursus: Matricide, averted and indirect matricide, patricide	8
4. Theseus and his parents and stepmother	18
5. The iconographical motif of a youth attacking a woman with a sword	29
6. Words, pictures and meanings	48
Abbreviations used in the text and not explained in the notes	59
Notes	61

Acknowledgments

I am grateful to Professor J. Boardman, and especially to Professors J.K. Davies and C.M. Robertson, who read an early draft of this paper and made helpful suggestions. My indebtedness to discussions about Theseus with Professor W.G. Forrest will be apparent in the text.

It so happened that at the time when the publication of this work was being discussed with the Institute, a study of Theseus from a different viewpoint by Professor J.P. Barron was also being prepared for publication. Each of us read the other's work, and the possibility of publishing both studies in one volume was considered. Eventually it was found to be practicable for the two works to appear separately, and for this one to go ahead. Acknowledgments to Professor Barron appear in the appropriate places below.

I should like to express my gratitude to Miss P.A. Winker, secretary of the School of Archaeology and Oriental Studies of Liverpool University, who very kindly typed the manuscript; to Mr J.M. Murphy for his assistance in preparing the work for publication; and to Miss Margaret Packer who is responsible for typesetting the volume.

For photographs I am indebted to the following: Dr X.S. Gorbounova of the Hermitage Museum, Leningrad, Dr R.A. Higgins and Mr B.F. Cook of the British Museum, Mr M.J. Vickers of the Ashmolean Museum, Oxford, Dr A.J.N.W. Prag of the Manchester Museum, and the Staatliche Antikensammlungen, Munich.

31 March 1979   Christiane Sourvinou-Inwood

List of Illustrations

Plate 1 a   Leningrad 649 (St. 830)
       b   Oxford 1920.103

Plate 2 a   Manchester iii.I.41
       b   Oxford 1966.508

Plate 3 a   London E 446
       b   Charlecote, Fairfax-Lucy Collection

Plate 4   Munich 2354 (J 243)

1. Preface

This study arose out of an initially limited investigation of a group of vases with scenes representing a youth attacking a woman with a sword, and usually interpreted as representing Theseus and his mother, Aithra. I became convinced that this interpretation is incorrect, and my research led me to consider in detail the relationship of Theseus with his parents and with his stepmother, Medea, and especially the motifs of tension and hostility inherent in these relationships. Such an investigation may properly be conducted only in the framework of a wider, if necessarily brief, investigation of the themes of tension and hostility between parent and child in Greek mythology. As a result, this essay has a central theme providing a backbone, and other units which, though related to the main theme in that they illuminate or provide a theoretical framework for it, are also self-contained in the sense that they stand or fall on their own: their validity does not depend on the argument of the main theme.

The central theme is provided by the group of vases showing Theseus attacking a woman and by the story they represent. I argue, on the correlation between two grids of evidence, iconographical and mythological, that they show the conflict between Theseus and his stepmother, Medea. The two grids are considered separately, in terms of their own rules and conventions, with the correlation at a subsequent stage. I consider this essential, given the fragmentary state of the evidence, to avoid the distortions that can arise from a synthetic approach. For example, if the iconographical reading of a scene tells us that it represents activity A, while from the literary sources we expect activity B, a separate study of the two grids will clearly bring out the contradiction, as is proper since it exists in the evidence as we have it. This is the result of the fragmentary state of our knowledge, and to disguise it is to corrupt the evidence. The synthetic approach, on the other hand, is likely to lead to, or at least to allow, a conscious or unconscious adaptation of the reading of the iconographical rendering – which, it must be stressed, can be as unambiguous as literary evidence – to create a tidy picture. In other words, the synthetic approach may lead to a corruption of what evidence we have, leading to a likely distortion of the overall reconstruction.

The next stage in the unfolding of the main theme is the consideration of the story of Theseus and Medea. I shall put forward a tentative reconstruction of the circumstances of its invention, its history, its reshaping and its significance and function. Clearly, this section does *not* depend on the last, in which I argued that the vase-scenes showing a youth attacking a woman depict Theseus and Medea. Whether or not this interpretation is correct, the story of Theseus' relationship with Medea is known from the literary sources, and my analysis of the theme and its significance could be valid even if my interpretation of the scenes is incorrect. In that case we should lose the chronological landmarks and the argument about the chronologically concentrated popularity of the subject provided by the vases.

The "self-contained" units woven into the study are the following: first, an investigation of the mythological themes involving intense hostility between parents and children, that is, matricide, averted and indirect matricide, and patricide; second, the relationship of Theseus and his parents. That with his mother interlocks with the main theme insofar as the vase-scenes have been interpreted by others as showing Theseus and his mother. The theme of Theseus' relationship with his father is closely related, for Medea acted against Theseus in collaboration with her husband, the hero's father Aigeus. Consideration of this theme also involves a discussion of the version of the myth which presents Theseus as the son of Poseidon. These themes are themselves considered in the context of the development of the whole Theseus legend as I see it.

My intention was that the study of this mythological nexus should also serve as an illustration of the way in which, in my opinion, Greek mythological mentality operated.

I realise that my methodology may appear objectionable both to some "traditional" and to some "progressive" students of mythology. In fact, I was made aware only recently of the fact that for some scholars the combination of different approaches in the study of myth is jarring. This came to me through the realisation that the fact that I had combined a typological consideration of Dark Age hand-made pottery with the use of a "structuralist" tool in the same paper aroused some suspicion. However, I will persist in my approach, which has been termed by a friend "eclectic". For it is only by applying to the mthyological material many different approaches and methodological tools that we can diminish the risk of distortion and illuminate as many aspects as possible. Myths are multidimensional phenomena, with many meanings and functions, both at the synchronic and at the diachronic level. And each methodological tool is likely to be best suited to extracting a certain specific set of meanings. Moreover, and partly because of the multidimensional character of myths, many sets of circumstances have impinged upon the myths, affecting their creation, transformation and shape, such as, for example, the historical circumstances or the way in which the myths are transmitted. Each set of circumstances should be investigated, to elucidate how they could and perhaps did affect the myth. But each should be investigated according to its own rules and techniques, according to its own methodology, not by extrapolating from the myths themselves or by making generic assumptions. Hence it is possible that something as mundane as the typology of hand-made Dark Age pottery may need to come into a mythological study.

Of course, "pure structuralists" believe, at least in theory, that the historical circumstances are irrelevant. I feel that they are relevant or not depending on the aim of the mythological study, on what one is trying to extract from a myth. If one is attempting to reconstruct a universal "mythological grammar and syntax" assuming that such a thing exists, if one is trying to find out how "les mythes se pensent dans les hommes" (C. Lévi-Strauss, *Mythologiques. Le Cru et le Cuit* [Paris 1964] 20), then historical circumstances probably are irrelevant. But if one is attempting to recover the significance, or rather the many levels of significance of a myth in a particular society, at a particular moment in time, then the historical and social perspective is essential. Unless the recovery of meanings and functions and their consideration is conducted in the framework of the specific context which produced them, and to which they referred, in terms of which the myths meant things and had functions, the mythological study becomes a mere intellectual game.

Consequently, I used a modified structuralist approach as *one* of the tools for illuminating myths, in combination with others, and when the mythological material warrants it.

So my approach is indeed eclectic. But, at least in intention, it is the eclecticism of the *Ara Pacis*, in which the different elements were deliberately selected, and which attempted to create something new in meaning as well as in form, rather than that of Pasiteles and his pupils.

2. Was Theseus a matricide manqué?

It would be difficult to deny that Theseus behaved negligently towards his father, Aigeus, whose death he caused by omission. But nothing in the literary tradition can support the accusation that he ever attempted to cause bodily harm to his mother, Aithra. To her, according to our literary sources, he was almost a model son — almost, since his habit of abducting women caused Aithra trouble and made her spend part of her declining years in foreign lands as a slave to Helen. However, Beazley's *ARV²* and Brommer's *Vasenlisten zur griechischen Heldensage*[3] tell a different story. According to them, some vases certainly, and others less certainly, carry representations of Theseus attacking his mother, Aithra, with a sword. True, the authors nowhere maintain (since the two books consist only of lists) that the hero intended to harm his mother. Indeed, some scholars discussing one of these scenes have attempted to pass off the whole episode as horseplay between mother and son. But the scenes speak for themselves: of all the representations interpreted as Theseus attacking Aithra with a sword, only one could remotely, and by stretching a point, be seen as rough horseplay. The rest are potent attacks with intent to kill. It should be noted here that Beazley and Brommer were not the originators of this slur on Theseus' character; the whole thing was started by a late archaic Athenian cup-painter called Makron.

Makron painted a scene in the tondo of one of his cups, now in Leningrad, Leningrad 649 (St. 830) (*ARV²* 460,13; here Plate 1a),[1] showing a youth wearing chiton, cloak and petasos, about to attack a woman with a sword he is drawing from its scabbard, and he inscribed these two characters "Theseus" and "Aithra". It is on the basis of this cup with the inscribed characters that the rest of the scenes have been interpreted as representing Theseus and Aithra. The argument behind this identification runs as follows.

In the uninscribed scenes, the youth is wearing a petasos, or more rarely a pilos, a cloak, and sometimes sandals. He may have a club, and is in general represented according to the Attic iconographical scheme used to represent Theseus. Therefore, he is, like Makron's youth attacking a woman, Theseus. Consequently, these scenes show, as does the Makron cup, Theseus attacking a woman with a sword, and are therefore likely to have the same subject as Makron's cup. We know from the inscriptions that this subject is Theseus attacking Aithra, therefore all the scenes in which a youth attacks a woman with a sword represent Theseus attacking Aithra.

This argument is valid, provided that all its consequences are followed up and taken into account. It should be kept in mind that the Makron cup diverges from the rest of the scenes here under discussion in composition and in the stances both of youth and woman, while on these points the other scenes show a remarkable consistency and homogeneity. This being the case, one of two things is possible. Either the subject is one and the same on Makron's cup and in the rest of the scenes, despite the iconographical difference; in which case it is legitimate to use the inscribed cup as evidence for the identification of the characters in the other scenes, but it is also necessary to interpret the subject in such a way that it "covers" both iconographical patterns. Or else the iconographical difference is significant, the two iconographical patterns expressing different subjects and therefore it is not legitimate to interpret the uninscribed scenes on the basis of the evidence provided by Makron's tondo.[2]

All the uninscribed scenes show, clearly and unequivocally, a youth attacking a woman with a sword. Therefore the problem of whether the Makron scene belongs with the rest hangs on whether it also shows Theseus attacking a woman with a sword or whether, on the contrary, those scholars are right who think that it represents Theseus and Aithra playing about proudly after the recovery of the sword from under the rock.[3] The Makron scene should therefore be considered in some detail.

It is first advisable, however, to create a theoretical framework for this consideration, by assessing the method on which it will be based. This will consist of examining the scene's individual iconographical elements and their combination, and establishing their meaning on the basis of the meanings which they have in scenes where it is unambiguous. The validity of such a decoding clearly depends on the degree of conventionality, or conversely of freedom, of the medium, Greek iconography; for conventionality, that is, codification, ensures consistency in the use of "signs". It cannot be doubted that Greek iconography does include a very considerable element of conventionality, operating, and to some extent conditioned by, the use of codified conventions. These can be simple, like the roving eye of Herakles and the attributes which identify specific gods or heroes, or more complex, like gestures and stances and their combination into a whole "scheme", for example, the abduction scheme. In Greek iconography most of these conventions are undoubtedly strongly motivated,[4] with a natural relation between the convention and that which it represents. But this motivation does not entail lack of convention; it does not alter the fact that these signs, however much motivated, are still codified ways of showing things, established and used in the framework of the whole code of Greek iconography.[5] For example, the fact that the scheme of erotic pursuit on Greek vessels is based on a natural scheme of pursuit does not alter the fact that it is a convention of Greek iconography that erotic pursuits are shown in this way. This conventional character makes easily intelligible the meaning of newly created scenes to those familiar with the whole system of conventions, that is, to the contemporary users of the vessels. This conventionality also entails that the "transmitter of the message", the vase-painter, is to some extent conditioned by the established convention so that in his iconographical thinking grief, for example, is equivalent to "head resting on outside of palm", and vice versa.

In these circumstances, it is clear that the method delineated above is valid; and that the correct way of decoding a scene is by considering its individual iconographical elements and the way in which they relate within the framework of our knowledge of the whole code of Greek iconography. *Ad hoc* interpretations imposed on the iconographical schemes are here more misleading than in most cases. Moreover, these considerations make it possible to suggest that similarity in the iconographical elements, and especially in the iconographical scheme of two or more scenes (that is, similarity in the *signifier*), should alert us to the possibility of similarity in the meaning of these scenes (that is, in the *signified*), even outside the highly codified scenes like abduction, erotic pursuit, and so on.[6] It is now time to turn to the detailed examination of Makron's tondo.

It is the earliest scene showing a youth attacking a woman with a sword — if that is what he is doing. It shows an adolescent in short chiton and chlamys, petasos slung at the back of his neck, drawing his sword from an elaborate scabbard and advancing fiercely towards a woman. A pair of spears is resting against the black background. As the youth advances towards her, the woman has shifted her weight to her left (back) leg, the one farther from the youth; her right (front) foot touches the ground only by the tip of its toes. This suggests to me that she is not advancing to meet the youth, but that she is starting to retreat before his advance. That is supported by the whole inclination of her body: its axis is oblique, inclined backwards, as if the woman has started retreating without having yet changed the position of her feet. Her right arm is extended towards the youth, and her right hand touches his chin; her left arm is also moving towards the youth; it is bent at the elbow, and the hand, very near the youth's face, is open, palm upwards, fingers extended. In Greek iconography these gestures, and especially the touching of the chin, are unmistakably gestures of supplication and entreaty. In fact, the gestures on this cup have been interpreted in this way by Neumann in his detailed study of gestures and gesticulation in Greek art: he is in no doubt that the woman is defined by her gestures as a suppliant.[7]

The "playful" interpretation suggested by Dugas and Flacelière is, I think, based on false iconographical assumptions. First, it is possible that, through a parallel with real life, the half-parted lips of the woman may be considered an indication of joy. That this is not so is clear when we consider that this type of half-parted lips is not uncommon in Makron's work for various types of figures and situations; indeed, Helen attacked by Menelaos in the scene on the skyphos Boston 13.186 (*ARV*[2] 458,1) has the same half-parted lips. Second, Dugas and Flacelière considered the fact that the woman has both arms extended as cancelling out the "supplication" significance of each individual arm and hand: they think that Aithra "lui tend les bras en joyeuse fierté".[8] However, the motif of both arms extended towards the aggressor in supplication is anything but rare in Greek iconography.[9] In Neumann's opinion the gesture of begging with both arms extended is used for two specific types of supplication.[10] First, in the representation of the supplication of those whose fate has not yet been decided at the moment of action depicted; and second, for figures who beg for mercy on behalf of others. If Neumann is right, this scene would, of course, fall in the first category.

Another element of the scene which has, in my opinion, been misinterpreted by Dugas and Flacelière and has contributed to the misinterpretation of the whole scene, is the role of the youth's sword. The two French scholars claim that Theseus is taking the sword from its scabbard to admire it in the sun. But the youth is not looking at the sword at all; he is looking intensely at the woman against whom he is purposefully advancing.[11]

In these circumstances, there can be little doubt that the scene does not show horseplay, but a serious attack. It may perhaps be objected that if there had been a story about a joke-attack on Aithra by Theseus, Makron could have used — as a joke? — the iconography of the serious attack, and altered its meaning precisely through the use of the inscribed names which said that it was that occasion of horseplay that was shown. However, I know of no parallel for such a process in Greek iconography. I know of no case in which the iconography of a scene shows that the subject is A while in fact it is meant to be B and the only way in which it is indicated that it is B, the only way in which the change of meaning is operated, is by an inscription, that is, by signs which in the code of Greek iconography are semiologically unimportant and usually absent.

The conclusion that the scene shows a serious, not a joke, attack, is confirmed by another argument. We saw above that similarity in the signifier between two or more scenes should alert us to the possibility of similarity in the signified; in other words, if the iconographical schemes are similar, the subjects and meanings of the scenes are also likely to be similar. A contemporary variant of the Makron scene, with different protagonists and unambiguous meaning, does indeed exist, and it denotes a serious attack: that of Odysseus on Circe on the cup Athens Acr. 293 by the Brygos Painter (ARV^2 369,5; Langlotz pls. 17–8). The tondo scene is not unlike the Makron scene in the upper part; but side B, also showing Odysseus attacking Circe, is almost the mirror image of Makron's tondo. The movement is in the opposite direction, and, of course, Odysseus the man is shown bearded unlike Theseus the youth. The stance of the two heroes is identical. Circe is also very similar to the woman on Makron's scene, with both hands outstretched, but her hand does not touch Odysseus' chin; so, if anything, Makron's scene denotes a more extreme case of serious attack, and more urgency in the supplication. Clearly, it is irrelevant which scheme, Makron's or the Brygos Painter's, came first.[12] What matters is that the same iconographical scheme was appropriate both for Odysseus attacking Circe and for the subject of Makron's tondo: the latter must represent a serious attack.

As it happens, there is a close and consistent similarity between the theme "Odysseus attacking Circe with a sword" and "Theseus attacking a woman with a sword": it will be seen below (n. 147) that the scheme which became canonical for "Theseus attacking a woman" is iconographically very close to the one normally used in red-figure for showing Odysseus attacking Circe. I shall argue that this close iconographical similarity corresponds to a close thematic similarity, going beyond the fact that both stories involve attacks.

It is clear that Makron's scene shows a serious attack and belongs with the rest of the scenes mentioned above which depict Theseus attacking with a sword a woman whom Makron named Aithra. Because no such attack is attested in the literary evidence, some scholars[13] have tried to water down, as it were, the meaning of the attack, by interpreting it as a forcible request by Theseus for the *gnorismata* — an episode, it should be noted, equally unknown to the literary tradition. This suggestion does not convince me for several reasons. First, once more, the iconographical scheme. It is too "extreme" to be portraying more or less vain threats in which both participants knew that no serious question of life and death was being decided. This is clear not so much from Theseus' stance as from the woman's: the gestures of the suppliant, including that of touching the aggressor's chin, are used only for truly serious cases of supplication.[14] The same "extreme" character suggestive of a serious attack is also found in most of the other scenes. If these scenes do indeed show Theseus forcibly requesting the *gnorismata* from Aithra, then a lost story must have existed in which Theseus managed to convince his mother that her life was in danger — although *ex hypothesi* he would have wanted Aithra alive, so that she would sooner or later guide him to the *gnorismata*. But there are other objections. If we judge from the *testimonia* concerning the rock episode and the recovery of the *gnorismata* that have survived, it would appear[15] that, according to the story which told of that part of Theseus' life, the young hero did not know about his father, the rock or the *gnorismata* until the moment at which his mother considered him to be grown up enough to hear the story of his birth and to be shown the rock under which lay the *gnorismata*. After that it was up to Theseus to lift the rock, and threatening Aithra was not going to help either way. Finally, Theseus in the Makron cup is armed with a sword and a couple of spears; elsewhere he has of course the sword, and he sometimes wears the sandals which were one of the *gnorismata* left by Aigeus under the rock. On the other hand, tradition implies that Theseus' sword has always been the sword which Aigeus hid for him under the rock, that which he obtained as a token of his manhood after he fulfilled the *dokimasia* of lifting the rock. Moreover, and most important, all the representations of Theseus lifting the rock show him totally unarmed. That would suggest that the first weapon he ever had was his father's sword. As a matter of fact, the representation of Theseus lifting the rock nearest in time to the Makron cup[16] also shows him without a petasos and undistinguishable from any other youth but for the context; it is after he has passed the *dokimasia* of lifting the rock that he will become Theseus the hero, shown with his usual paraphernalia. In later representations he already wears the petasos and sometimes the sandals in scenes where he is lifting the rock; but he is always unarmed.[17] Our scenes, which show Theseus in possession of and using the sword, must belong to a moment subsequent to its recovery from under the rock. They cannot be showing Theseus forcibly claiming the *gnorismata* from his mother.

It may be objected that this argument does not take into account the "synoptical" character of some Greek scenes, the fact that sometimes the vase-painter can combine elements from two or more moments of the story and weave them into one scene. But this "synoptical" character can have no relevance to the sword here, although it could easily have explained the presence of the sandals if the sword had been absent. If we were to consider the scene as telling a story "synoptically", we would have to take the presence of the sword, which properly belongs to a subsequent moment of the story, as meant to hint at what the quarrel was about. But in all our scenes the sword is not a parenthetic, additional, element, but that on which the whole action hinges — an element without which the whole character of the action would radically be altered. Makron's scene without the sword or without any weapons, would not be portraying a deadly danger, and the woman's serious supplication would be out of place. The rest of the scenes, those following the pattern of the pursuit of a woman fleeing in terror, without the drawn sword, would automatically become scenes of erotic pursuit. It is thus highly implausible that the scenes represent Theseus forcibly claiming the *gnorismata* from his mother.

Was there in fact a story in which Theseus attacked his mother with a sword with intent to kill, or at least to inflict serious pain on her? The answer is no, not in the existing literary sources. Nor are there, in the literary sources, any circumstances in which any occasion for a matricidal attack could have arisen. However, since the literary sources are far from complete, this in itself does not mean much. But there is another way of approaching the problem. The themes of matricide and attempted matricide in Greek mythology can be considered to ascertain whether there is a basic thematic structure common to all. If this is the case, the legend of Theseus cannot have contained a now lost matricide story unless the basic thematic structure of matricide or attempted matricide fits into, and is consistent with, the extant part of his legend. In this study it will be found that the motif "hostility to the parent" does occur in the legend of Theseus, but that it is the father to whom it is referred, and not to the mother. This fact will emerge clearly from the study of the themes which make up the motif: matricide, indirect matricide, averted matricide and patricide. The study of these themes in the next chapter has several functions. First, it will show that neither matricide nor any of its variants is likely to have been contained in the legend of Theseus — and as a consequence that the Makron cup is unlikely to be showing Theseus attacking Aithra. Second, it will provide a brief study of these important mythological themes. And finally, the most important function, it will create the conceptual framework necessary to set in place and to appreciate fully the theme of the attempted murder of Theseus by his father and his stepmother which is central to this study, and which, as I shall argue, is reflected in the scenes showing Theseus attacking a woman with a sword.

3.   Excursus: matricide, averted and indirect matricide, patricide

The Greek myths dealing with matricide have been studied by M. Delcourt.[18] She argues that, apart from the two cases of clear and unequivocal matricide, those of Orestes and Alcmeon, Greek mythology contains stories in which matricide lurks hidden and disguised. These are legends in which the theme of hostility to the mother is underlying, but matricide is not committed. This she calls "matricide censuré".[19] Oidipous' victory over the Sphinx, for example, is, for Delcourt, a case of censored matricide.

Clearly, this type of classification depends on the assumption that the essence of the theme of matricide is hostility to the mother, and that whenever such hostility can be detected in a myth, in whatever form, it should be classified as "matricide" which has taken a different form because of moral censorship. I do not share this one-dimensional view of myths, and so shall examine the themes of the murder and indirect and averted murder of the parent with the purpose of elucidating their structure, the mentality which shaped them, and their significance. In the process I shall also be creating a conceptual framework against which to place the consideration of the relationship of Theseus, his parents and his stepmother. At the end, I shall survey very briefly Delcourt's categories. I should note that her indirect matricide and averted matricide categories overlap with my own, although I approach them differently and reach different conclusions.

First, **matricide**. The story of Orestes is attested in several variants.[20] Their comparison reveals that several themes are basic to the story, though they may appear in "stronger" or "weaker" versions, or may be duplicated. The thematic pattern of the story relevant to matricide is:

1. Agamemnon, Orestes' father, is murdered, either by Klytaimestra herself, or by her lover Aigisthos with her connivance and/or help. So whatever her precise role, Klytaimestra always causes the death of her husband.

2. A theme which is sometimes absent[21] is the danger to Orestes after Agamemnon's murder: either Aigisthos or Klytaimestra herself plans to murder him, but he is spirited away by his nurse or by his sister Elektra.

3. Also sometimes absent is the theme of the consultation of the Delphic oracle: Orestes is advised by Apollo to avenge his father by killing his mother.

4. Orestes kills his mother and her lover.

5. He is polluted by the murder of his mother and wanders, pursued by the Erinyes.[22]

6. His definitive purification and deliverance from the Erinyes encounters serious difficulties. It succeeds in the end, thanks to the divine help of Apollo.[23]

Alcmeon's matricide is also attested in several sources.[24] In all but two versions (for which there are two fourth-century variants, see previous note), the thematic pattern relevant to matricide runs:

1. Eriphyle betrays her husband Amphiaraos and causes his death.[25]

2. Amphiaraos orders his son Alcmeon to avenge him by killing his mother Eriphyle.

3. In some variants Eriphyle also endangers Alcmeon's life.

4. In some variants Alcmeon consults the Delphic oracle and Apollo advises him to kill his mother.[26]

5. He kills his mother.

6. He is polluted, becomes mad and wanders about pursued by the Erinyes.[27]

7. His final purification and deliverance from pollution is a long process fraught with difficulties. It finally succeeds thanks to divine help which takes different forms in the different variants; in all but one Alcmeon is said to have consulted the Delphic oracle and to have found deliverance thanks to Apollo's advice.[28] Asklepiades[29] says that "the gods" delivered him from the *nosos* because he killed his mother "ὁσίως ἀπαμύνοντα τῷ πατρί".

It is clear, then, that the two thematic patterns are extremely close, to the extent that we can speak of **the** thematic pattern, **the** structure of the matricide myth. There is only one theme which is found in the one story but not in the other: Alcmeon's father ordered his son to avenge him by killing his mother, a theme which would have been impossible to include in the overall myth of Agamemnon, Klytaimestra and Orestes, and which provides an additional sanction for the matricide in the story of Alcmeon, an explicification of his duty to his father. That means that the difference is insignificant. It is interesting to note that in both stories the same two themes fail to appear in all the versions: a) the mother also endangering her son's life, and b) the consultation of the Delphic oracle before the matricide and Apollo's advice to kill the mother. This may indicate that the two themes are secondary and "dispensable", and not basic to the matricide myth. A closer consideration suggests that this is indeed the case, for a) is a strong and explicit version of the hostility of the mother towards the son which is involved already in the murder of the father, but in a less direct and less explicit form: that murder deprived the son of his father (see Aesch., *Eumen.* 600–2), and placed on him the obligation of vengeance with its ensuing miseries.[30] With regard to b), it may rightly be observed that the Delphic oracle intruded in many legends because of its special position in the Greek world from the eighth century. But this is not necessarily the only reason why it appears in this myth. Of course, in the second part of the story, the Delphic Apollo is the natural agent for providing the divine help needed. he *par excellence* is the god concerned with purification on the one hand, and with restoring or establishing order on the other. (Why divine help should be forthcoming to matricides will be considered below). In my opinion, once Apollo and the oracle appear thus, supporting the matricide after the crime, they can easily, as a next step, be made to legitimate it in advance, by a process of intensification and polarisation natural to the mythological mentality. So theme b) can be seen as a derivative, polarised version of the idea that Apollo (or "the god") are on the side of the matricide.

Thus the basic thematic structure of the matricide myth is:

1. The mother causes the death of her husband, and is hostile, directly or indirectly, to her son.

2. The son kills her.

3. He is polluted, driven mad, and pursued by the Erinyes.

4. His purification and deliverance is difficult, but finally achieved through divine help.

Running through this myth, and stated explicitly in Aeschylus' *Oresteia*, is a basic antithesis, a dialectical relationship between two contradictory concepts: Order and Disorder, at the level of the individual and at the level of society. This is not coincidental but meaningful, as is shown first by the consistency and the multidimensionality of the antithesis; and second by the fact that Order-Disorder is an extremely significant opposition in Greek thought and society. This basic opposition is analysed into the following pairs of opposed motifs, each also significant in Greek society and thought:

At the social level: Loyalty to one's oikos — Disloyalty to one's oikos

　　　　　　　　　　Social order — Social disorder

At the religious level: Purity — Pollution
 (and associated with it, at the physiological level:
　　　　　　　　　　Sanity — Insanity)

Another pair of motifs in opposition, at right angles to the previous set, is: Divine help-Divine persecution and divine punishment; and, associated with it, Upper gods-Nether gods.[31]

The themes of the myth relate to those opposing pairs as follows:

	Disloyalty to oikos Social disorder Pollution	Loyalty to oikos Social order Purity, avoidance of pollution
	Wife kills husband (which also means son's father — for this double aspect, Aesch. *Eum.* 600–2)	
	Son kills mother. He thus incurs pollution, is in a state of *mania*,	Son avenges father by killing mother. By doing this he avoids pollution (for example, Aesch. *Choeph.* 269–92).
Divine persecution	and is pursued by the Erinyes.	The Erinyes persecute the matricide (to punish the person who brought disorder and pollution is to serve the cause of order).
Divine help	The gods, and Apollo in particular, help and protect the matricide, thus taking the side of the disturber of the social order.	The gods, and Apollo in particular, help and protect the matricide because he disturbed order only to restore the order that had already been upset.
		The matricide is purified and freed from *mania* and the Erinyes.

Another pair of opposites also run through the myth, parallel to and closely connected with the pair Order-Disorder: it is the opposition male-female, meaningful not only at the physiological level, but in Greek society and thought also extremely important at the social, political and cultural levels.[32] In Greek myth, this opposition is frequently used as a vehicle for expressing opposites of a higher order.[33] It is consistent with this Greek mentality that the female corresponds to disorder, the male to order. And in the matricide myth it is the female who initiates the disorder, and the male who finally overcomes it. But in the intermediate stages the roles have become mixed, corresponding to the contradictions to be overcome.

It is clear that this myth contains basic contradictions. The act of matricide is at once one of loyalty to the oikos and of disloyalty to it. It restores social order by punishing and eliminating the generator of disorder, and itself brings about new disorder.[35] It both avoids and incurs pollution; it stimulates both divine help and divine persecution and punishment. In their turn, the motifs of divine help and divine punishment are also ambivalent. The former puts the gods on the side of a criminal and the generator of disorder, but this is just and serves to uphold order since the matricide committed his crime in the cause of justice and order. The divine persecution by the Erinyes brings disorder, wandering and insanity, but it does so to punish disorder, so that order should be upheld. These contradictions are the inevitable result of the initial disturbance of order by the mother, through the murder of her husband.[36] They are finally overcome through the successful purification of the son, which restores order.

The murder of the husband which triggered the disasters is clearly an act of hostility against the husband and indirectly also against the son. Hostility against both husband and son is equivalent to hostility against and disloyalty to the husband's oikos.[37] If we concentrate for the moment on this aspect of the myth, and consider the murder of the husband as a polarised version of hostility and disloyalty to the husband's oikos we can recover for the theme of "family tensions" the following mentality: "if a woman is disloyal to her husband's oikos, catastrophe will follow, the values of society will be upset, and only with the greatest difficulty will order be restored for the second generation, the son". The fact that the disloyalty to the husband's oikos takes the polarised form of the murder of the husband triggers another theme within the matricide myth: the vengeance of kin which perpetuates pollution (Aesch., *Choeph.* 400–4). This theme too takes a polarised form in the myth: the murderer is herself a blood relative, indeed herself a parent. Dodds, referring to the *Oresteia,* puts it this way: "the logic of the vendetta, brought to the test of this limiting case, breaks down in flat contradiction".[38] And this acknowledgement of the inherently contradictory character of the law of the vengeance of kin, made explicit through its polarisation in the context of this "family tension" myth, is another "message" of the matricide myth and another aspect of the mentality which shaped it. (It should not be overlooked that apart from this myth's major themes there are others minor only insofar as they do not belong exclusively to matricide, or more generally myths of "family tensions", for example, the theme of pollution and the mentality behind it.) The last primary dimension of the matricide myth is the creation of mythological representations (again polarised, since myth is the subject under discussion) of psychological family tensions,[39] the feelings of veiled hostility and the conflicts which arise within the family. For Delcourt,[40] this is the essence of the matricide myth: the hostility to the mother which symbolizes and expresses the young man's struggle to free himself from his childhood, which is associated with his mother and the women's sphere. But myths are not confined to one "basic meaning". They are not static translations of a concept into narrative but dynamic multidimensional vehicles on which operate, depending on the themes involved, different types of "mentality" in the sense of ideological mould pattern of beliefs, in which the narrative material is cast and shaped. (This "mentality" is, of course, to be distinguished from the basic mythological mentality, the mythological grammar, which produces, for example, a polarisation of situations, and which for the structuralists is based on a model of binary opposites.) It is precisely because of this dynamic character and this multidimensionality that myths could be reshaped and/or reinterpreted, or an additional dimension added, to express the preoccupations of a specific historical moment. Even when one "meaning" may appear to be of more central importance, the myth cannot and must not be considered as equivalent to a narrative expression of that "meaning". I have suggested that in the myth of matricide, in all its versions and variants, three basic types of mentality (in the sense of "ideological mould") can be recovered, corresponding to three basic themes: disloyalty to the husband's oikos; law of the vengeance of kin; and psychological conflicts within the family. Of course, individual authors treating a specific variant can make it express many other "messages" and ideologies by enriching and adding further dimensions to the basic structure.

The theme "disloyalty to the husband's oikos" is, not surprisingly, closely related with and complementary to the messages of, and mentalities behind, the other myths of the thematic category "family tensions": patricide, indirect matricide and averted matricide. Not surprisingly, since the basic ideology behind all those myths is expressive of the social realities and beliefs about the family in Greek society. The theme of "disloyalty to the husband's oikos" was touched upon by Delcourt,[41] who saw it in a restricted form and gave it a restricted significance and range of operation in these myths. The only form she detected is that generated by the rival loyalty to the brother or brothers, as is the case with Eriphyle and with Althaia in a myth of indirect matricide.[42] Delcourt thinks that in these two cases we have a conflict between the archaic concept according to which a woman is tied to the genos of her birth, and the later system in which she is primarily her husband's spouse. The evidence as to whether in archaic Greece a woman did indeed owe first allegiance to the oikos or genos of her birth is inconclusive. But in any case this would not be the only form a woman's disloyalty to her husband's oikos could take: adultery is an obvious alternative. The analysis of the myth of matricide suggested that fear of this disloyalty and its disastrous consequences was the major preoccupation; the conflict between loyalty to her family of birth and loyalty to her husband's oikos would be only one aspect of that danger. It is clearly beyond the present scope to consider the *Oresteia.*[43] Aeschylus, of course, has impregnated the basic structure of the myth of matricide with many higher meanings, and the conflicts involved are multidimensional.[44]

I shall deal now with the other myths in this nexus, although not considering each in all its variants, unless they involve the theme of the murder or averted murder of the parent. Consideration of the different variants of the myth of Telephos for example, will clearly throw light on that specific myth, its historical development, and so on, while here I am concerned with one theme (patricide, averted matricide or indirect matricide) as manifested in *its* different variants in the different myths.[45]

Indirect matricide, as defined by Delcourt, is the story in which the son does not kill his mother, but the mother commits suicide after having caused the death of her son.[46] There is only one case of clear and unadulterated indirect matricide:[47] that of Althaia and Meleager. The Oidipous myth contains a variant of indirect matricide, interwoven with and defined by the main theme of the patricide and its consequence and that of Phaidra and Hippolytos is a version of indirect matricide with the stepmother replacing the mo

The story of Althaia and Meleager survives in several versions.[49] In most Althaia is said to have caused her son's death.[50] The basic lines of the myth[51] are:

1. Meleager kills his mother's brothers.[52]
2. Because of this, Althaia causes Meleager's death.[53]
3. Meleager dies.
4. Althaia commits suicide.

Althaia has not only shown hostility to her son but has also been disloyal to her husband's oikos, since she seriously harmed that oikos — through the death of her son because of a rival loyalty to her brothers. That aspect of the myth becomes more explicit in the versions in which Meleager kills his uncles during a war between Meleager's people, the Aetolians, and the Kouretes, in which they are on opposite sides.

This disloyalty to the husband's oikos also appears in the myth of Phaidra and Hippolytos,[54] which involves hostility to the stepson. The basic themes of this myth relevant to "indirect stepmatricide"[55] run as follows:

1. Phaidra falls in love with her stepson Hippolytos, thus being disloyal to her husband and threatening his oikos with disintegration.
2. Hippolytos refuses her, thus showing loyalty to his father and to his oikos.
3. Phaidra falsely accuses Hippolytos to Theseus, and attributes to him her own disloyalty.
4. Theseus causes the death of his son Hippolytos.
5. Phaidra commits suicide.

Consequently, it appears that the theme of indirect matricide contains the same "message" as that of matricide (also in a polarised form): if a woman is disloyal to her husband's oikos, catastrophe will follow. With regard to the "psychological" dimension of the myth, we must distinguish between indirect matricide and indirect stepmatricide. The former gives a polarised mythological expression to the same detachment from the mother associated with dawning manhood as matricide, but also, as in matricide, to the mother's detachment from and even resentment of the son who has become an independent man. Indirect stepmatricide may, as Delcourt thinks, also include a "censored" version of the mother-son "hostility" insofar as it is a transformation of indirect matricide. But it certainly gives a mythological expression to feelings which can be generated in a stepmother-stepson relationship: a stepmother's resentment of her stepchild, and a possible sexual dimension in the relationship. Indirect matricide, like matricide, also includes a polarised expression of the inherent limitations and contradictions of the vendetta: Althaia avenged her brothers by "killing" her son, and ended up by killing herself. Clearly, indirect matricide is closely related on the one hand to matricide and on the other to indirect stepmatricide, forming a link between them.

In the latter, however, the disloyalty to the husband's oikos is manifested through murderous hostility against the person of the son; for this reason, in this myth, there is no final redemption for anyone. Since the son is the future of the oikos, his destruction means catastrophe.

In **averted matricide** the son attacks his mother with intent to kill while both are ignorant of the relationship between them. Then recognition occurs and matricide is avoided. The theme survives in two versions, the myths of Ion and Kreousa and of Telephos and Auge.

The story of Ion and Kreousa is known only from Euripides' play. Pearson[56] suggests that before it was used by the tragedians, "the history of Ion's parentage was only preserved orally in connection with the local worship of Apollo at Athens". And he notes that, since only Euripides' version survives, we cannot know which details were Euripides' invention and which were part of the common stock.

The basic lines of the story are:

1. Ion is born of the love of Kreousa and Apollo.
2. Kreousa exposes him.
3. Apollo causes him to be brought up at Delphi by the Pythia.
4. Kreousa marries Xouthos; they have no children and decide to consult the Delphic oracle about it.
5. Apollo tells Xouthos that Ion is his (Xouthos') son. Xouthos intends to take him into his home and recognises him as such.
6. Kreousa attempts to poison Ion.
7. An accidental/miraculous event reveals the plot.
8. Ion is about to take revenge by killing Kreousa.
9. Recognition occurs, the matricide is averted.

Clearly the hostility starts on the mother's side: Kreousa first abandons Ion as a baby, then attempts to poison him.

The story of Telephos and Auge has the same basic structure. It survives in many versions.[57] Of the two basic variants, one involves the exposure of Telephos as a baby, and hence the subsequent averted matricide: it also has several versions. The basic lines of the story relevant to averted matricide are:

1. Auge's father received an oracle which said that Auge's son would kill his own sons (that is, Auge's brothers).
2. He took steps to prevent her from having a child.
3. Nevertheless, she bears Telephos by Herakles.
4. She exposes him on Mount Parthenion.
5. Telephos does not perish. In some versions he is suckled by a hind. He is brought up by the shepherds of King Korythos or by the King himself.
6. He does kill his mother's brothers.[58]
7. On the advice of the oracle[59] he goes to Mysia.
8. Auge's adopted father Teuthras wants to marry her to Telephos.[60]
9. Auge, who is averse to the marriage, intends to kill Telephos in the bridal chamber.
10. A miracle (a serpent comes between them) frustrates her and makes her confess.
11. Telephos is about to kill her in revenge.
12. Recognition occurs, and the matricide is averted.

It is clear that in both "averted matricide" myths the hostility starts with the mother: she exposes her son as a baby, and later tries to kill him. In both catastrophe is averted, and there is a happy ending, and in both the meeting between mother and son is brought about by the Delphic oracle. So the "message" contained in the theme is that the neglect and hostility of the mother towards her son does not have fatal consequences: catastrophe is averted and all ends well.[61] This "message" is complementary to that contained in the related theme of patricide (also concerned with the parent-child relationship and not involving the whole oikos as do matricide and indirect matricide).

Naked **patricide**, without any attenuating circumstances, is found only in the Theogonies. In legend there are three cases in which the son kills the father in ignorance of the relationship: Oidipous and Laios, Telegonos and Odysseus, and Althaimenes and Katreus. The basic lines of these stories relevant to patricide are:

Oidipous and Laios[62]	Telegonos and Odysseus[63]	Althaimenes and Katreus[64]
Laios received an oracle that his son would kill him. He tried to avoid having children.	Odysseus received an oracle that his son would kill him. He took precautions against Telemachos.	Katreus received an oracle that one of his children would kill him. *OR* (below).
Oidipous is born, his parents have him exposed.	[Odysseus had abandoned Circe – and Telegonos – before the oracle.]	
He is rescued by shepherds and brought up by the King of Corinth as his own son.		
	Telegonos is informed by Circe that his father is Odysseus. Telegonos sets off to find him.	
He consults the oracle about his parentage and is told that he will kill his father and marry his mother.		*OR*: Althaimenes received an oracle that he would kill his father.
He abandons Corinth which he considers his native city.		He leaves Crete, to avoid patricide, and settles in Rhodes.
		In Apollodoros he kills his sister who went with him.
He quarrels with Laios, not realising that he is his father.	Telegonos lands on Ithaca and fights with the inhabitants who are helped by Odysseus.	After a while, Katreus sets out to bring back Althaimenes; he lands on Rhodes and becomes involved in a fight with the natives who are joined by Althaimenes. Althaimenes is not aware of the newcomer's identity: either (Diod.) it was dark, or (Ap.) the natives could not hear Katreus' explanations because of the barking of dogs.
Oidipous kills Laios: **patricide**.	Telegonos kills Odysseus in ignorance of the relationship between them: **patricide**.	Althaimenes kills Katreus without recognising him: **patricide**.
	He realises that he has committed patricide and mourns Odysseus.	He realises that he has committed patricide and either (Apoll.) prayed and disappeared into a chasm, or (Diod.) shunned human society, wandering in deserted places until he dies from grief.[67]
He marries his mother.	He marries his father's wife, Penelope.	
Disaster to the city, revelation, catastrophe.[65]		
Ultimately he is heroized.	Circe sends Telegonos and Penelope to the Isles of the Blest.[66]	He became the recipient of heroic cult according to Diod. In Apollod. this is not mentioned but the disappearance into a chasm is equivalent to heroization.

In two of the three myths the hostility originates with the father, as in other myths involving some form of murder or averted murder of the parent. In the surviving myth of Althaimenes and Katreus no such hostility from father to son can be found. But it is known only from two later mythographical sources, and there is some reason for thinking (n. 67) that the original pattern[68] has been manipulated and altered. The variants as to who received the oracle and what precisely it contained could indicate corruption, or rather moral censorship, of the earlier myth. That impression is reinforced by other elements: the fact that in one version Katreus sends his other children away from the island; and Katreus' conviction that he could, if he wished, bring back Althaimenes to Crete. All this indicates that in the original story it had been Katreus who expelled Althaimenes from Crete.

If this is correct, the very basic pattern of the theme of patricide runs as follows: abandonment of or hostility to the son on the part of the father leads to catastrophe; the father is killed; the son, who is the victim of circumstance, suffers in life, but is heroized after death.[69]

The themes of patricide and averted matricide are clearly very closely related. They are parallel but reversed themes: the former ends in catastrophe, the latter in recognition, reconciliation and restoration of normal relationships. The composite "message" contained in the two myths is: "If a mother abandons her child and does not care for it, the consequences are not going to be catastrophic. If a father does this, disaster will follow."[70] This "message" is significant because the mentality it expresses corresponds to the realities of Greek society. In particular, it was a social reality, in Athens at least, that a child was totally and absolutely dependent on his father's goodwill. It was completely in the father's power whether or not to admit a new-born baby in the family, even if it was his legitimate offspring. He could choose instead to expose it.[71] If the child was found and nurtured by another person, it could be treated as slave or free at the discretion of the finder. But the father retained legal ties with the child, which could be revived, and the finder could not adopt it since adoption had to be transacted between the adopter and the child's father or his representative.[72] The father, of course, could also have his son adopted.[73] Even after the son came of age, it seems that the father had a continuing right to remove him from the house ($\dot{\alpha}\pi o\kappa\eta\rho\acute{u}\tau\tau\epsilon\iota\nu$). This would cut off the son from family worship, exclude him from the inheritance of his father's property, and make it difficult for him to defend his citizenship against an attack.[74] It is thus not difficult to see why the fear that the father may choose not to care for his son was an acute preoccupation which found expression in myth.

The myth of patricide also provides a polarised narrative expression for another social principle, this time of universal validity:[75] "for society to go on, sons must destroy (replace) their fathers". The same mythological representation, the murder of the father, also "represents" the psychological rivalry and conflict between father and son. Among the secondary[76] motifs interwoven into the myth of patricide (and once in averted matricide) is that of the inescapable oracle, which is moulded by the conviction that mortals can not foil destiny.[77]

The story of Oidipous includes indirect matricide. The hostility originates with the mother, since Oidipous had been abandoned by both parents, and rebounds on the mother. All the disasters which led to her suicide were the consequences of that initial abandonment. But since the primary theme of patricide defines the myth, it is Iokaste's incest with her son which provokes her suicide, not the son's death.[78]

It is interesting to note that in the case of Althaimenes, who had not been abandoned as a baby and who therefore knew his father, as his father knew him and knew where to find him, another factor replaces ignorance of identity and allows the patricide to take place: "noise", in the sense of interference in communication. In Apollodorus' version it was noise in the literal sense: the barking of dogs which prevented the Rhodian cowherds from hearing Katreus' explanations and understanding that he was not a pirate. In Diodorus' version, Katreus landed in the dark and we are to understand that this prevented Althaimenes from seeing and recognising him. It is likely that in the original version the "noise" consisted both of the barking of dogs and of darkness.

A more complex theme, a variation on the elementary patterns of the themes of murder and averted murder of the parent, is found in Sophocles' *Thyestes*.[79] Here the thematic pattern is double-decked: there are two parent-child relationships, with Pelopeia, the daughter/mother, as a pivot between the two men, Thyestes and his son/grandson Aigisthos. Thyestes holds the role of the father in both. The role of the child is first held by Pelopeia, who attracts the hostility of the parent (rape). Subsequently, the role is held by Aigisthos, who is about to commit patricide. But Pelopeia also to some extent takes on the part of the "guilty" parent which by right does not belong to her but to Thyestes. In the simple patricide theme, the "guilty" father who initiated the hostility against the child is killed; in the simple averted matricide theme, the mother is saved from death by recognition. Here the guilty **father's** murder is averted by recognition, of a sword. And the mother, who had **not** initiated the hostility but had been on the receiving end of it at the hands of the guilty father, attracts the punishment which should have gone to the guilty father, death. It is not death at the hands of her child, which could not be reconciled with the plots, but self-inflicted death, suicide. The thematic pattern runs:

1. Hostility against the child[1] (no recognition): Thyestes rapes Pelopeia.
2. Aggression of the child[2] against the parent: Aigisthos intends to kill Thyestes.
3. Recognition.
4. Averted patricide but also death of the mother.

So at 4 there is an inversion of the situations of the simple patricide and averted matricide themes. The patricide has been averted, as in the averted matricide, and not consumed, as in patricide. And it is the mother who dies, although she had not been involved in 2 and had been the victim in 1.[80] Another complex theme, of no immediate concern here, is the murder of the mother's stepmother.[81] There are two instances: Pelias and Neleus killed their mother's stepmother Sidero; and Amphion and Zethos killed Dirce, who had assumed the role of wicked stepmother towards their mother Antiope. The latter story includes an averted matricide which, though contained in a complex pattern, is itself simple: the exposure of the children by the mother is the initial act of hostility which triggers the story, recognition takes place at the fatal meeting, so matricide is averted.

I shall now survey briefly Delcourt's categories of matricide. She considers the theme a mythological representation of a hostility to the mother expressing the young man's struggle to free himself from his childhood and from the "contraintes familiales". So she classifies as "censored matricide" any myth that can be seen as a representation of this struggle. She distinguishes five categories.

(a) *Symbolic matricide.* Hephaistos imprisoned Hera on a magic throne. Delcourt thinks that magic immobility "est une litote de la mort". This it may be, and certainly a mother-son hostility is involved, but the myth is more complex. For the parent-child hostility, the mentality behind it is the same as in other themes considered above. The hostility originates with the mother, who rejects her baby son, and all eventually ends well. Abandonment of the baby by the mother does not end in disaster.

(b) *Indirect matricide.* At the morphological and classificatory level this is the same as the indirect matricide studied above.

(c) *Matricide avoided at the last moment.* From a classificatory and morphological point of view, the same as "averted matricide" above. Delcourt thinks that if more fifth-century tragedies had been preserved there would be several more cases of averted matricide. She rightly considers averted matricide a thematic element of the motif of the princess seduced or raped by a god, who exposes her child, only to come face to face with him later; the erstwhile exposed baby is now an adolescent whom his mother does not recognise.

(d) *Replacement of the mother by the stepmother.* This is not a thematic category but one of form of censure, its validity depending on Delcourt's assumption that the hostility of the mother is the starting point and the essence of these myths. I have already expressed my disagreement with this restricted view. In the psychological dimension, I am prepared to accept that the "psychological image" expressed and polarised in the myths involving a stepmother could conceivably include (although never exclusively) psychological representations of mother-son tensions. Morphologically, of the three myths Delcourt places in this category, one is the story of Phaidra and Hippolytos which has here been considered a variant of indirect matricide. The others are the complex stories of the murder of the mother's stepmother mentioned above.

(e) Delcourt argues that *the equivalence of the terrible mother with a monster to be defeated* is among the symbolic representations of the youth's struggle to free himself from his childhood and its associated mother. Thus she considers Oidipous' victory over the Sphinx as synonymous with and equivalent to his union with his mother which ended in her death.[82] This interpretation clearly depends on a one-dimensional view of myth. The struggle of a hero with a monster is not matricide in any sense. It could be that one "message" or mythological representation included in matricide myths may be similar to one of those found in the theme of victory over a monster if it is correct that the latter can also be seen as a symbol of the youth freeing himself from his childhood and from the "contraintes familiales".[83]

To recapitulate. Each theme dealing with the murder, indirect, or averted murder, of the parent has a common basic thematic structure in all its variants. In all the themes, the hostility, in whatever form, originates with the parent, a fact already noted by Delcourt. Each theme has crystallised and polarised in the form of mythological representations, different aspects of psychological and social family tensions. Each theme in all its versions, and each version in all its variants, carries the same "message" in the sense of being shaped by the same mentality and beliefs about social realities, whatever other motifs are interwoven with it and whatever other messages it may carry. The "messages" carried by these themes are also consistent. If a woman is disloyal to her husband's oikos, disaster will follow. If a father abandons and/or does not care for his son, disaster will follow. If a mother abandons her son, no fatal consequences will ensue. These "messages" express social realities of Greek life, and the fact that they have shaped these myths, and are thus "transmitted" through them, reinforces these realities and to some extent even perpetuates their acceptance and the validity of the institutions which generated them.

4. Theseus and his parents and stepmother

It is already apparent that the legend of Theseus cannot have contained a lost story of matricide or averted matricide. First, the necessary ingredient of all myths which involve a parent-child hostility is absent: the parent who attracts hostility is the one who, in some way or other, initiated it. This Aithra never did nor could have done given the framework of the surviving legend. I should stress that I am here concerned with the Attic myth of Theseus as it had developed from the late sixth century onwards. Although frequently remodelled and reinterpreted, it preserved the same basic thematic framework: the Troezenian childhood, the deeds on the road to Athens, and so on. Clearly it is this Attic myth that is reflected in fifth century Athenian iconography, not, for example, the eighth century Troezenian version. Second, the theme of actual matricide is triggered by the death of the son's father caused by his wife, the son's mother. Aithra cannot have caused Aigeus' death: such a story would be in complete contradiction with the extant legend. Moreover, Aigeus was not Aithra's husband; the motif of the mother's disloyalty to her husband's oikos, which is an ingredient of matricide, is thus necessarily absent. Nor does indirect matricide have a place in the legend of Theseus. Even if it had, it could not account for Makron's representing Theseus attacking Aithra; but it would have born witness to an underlying hostility between the two in the legend. However, this theme cannot have been part of the legend. Aithra never caused any harm to Theseus, let alone his death, nor were there any circumstances, in the framework of the known legend of Theseus, in which she could have committed such an action. There is thus no initial murderous action, or even impulse, directed against the son, to rebound upon the mother and make her commit suicide.[84]

As for averted matricide, its necessary precondition is that the mother should have abandoned her son as a baby. Such a situation cannot be fitted into the framework of Theseus' legend; it is in total contradiction with it. It was an essential part of the Attic myth that Theseus should have been brought up by Aithra at Troezen and then sent by her to his father in Athens. More will be said on this below. As will be seen, in the original Troezenian legend Theseus' father was probably Poseidon, and only Poseidon. In the context of that version Aithra could well have abandoned Theseus as a baby; and a meeting - attempted matricide - recognition sequence may well have followed. However, this is clearly irrelevant to Attic myth and the Attic iconography which reflects it, more so in the case of Theseus than in any other. Moreover, I shall argue that the Athenian and the Troezenian versions had been harmonised at an early stage. Clearly, this is the point at which to consider in some detail the problem of Theseus' parentage. It is his father's identify which is controversial; his mother is always said to be Aithra.

Theseus is sometimes said to be the son of Aigeus, the Athenian king, sometimes that of Poseidon. Heroes are generally descendants of gods. They can be divided into three categories: a) heroes with two mortal parents, for instance Hector and Agamemnon; b) heroes with one divine and one mortal (mother) parent, for instance, Achilles and Minos; c) heroes with a mortal mother and two putative fathers, one mortal and one divine, as Herakles and Theseus.

Parentage of type a) follows the natural physiological model. That of type b) could be called "heroic" *par excellence*, for it is expressive of the nature of the hero. Heroes are ambivalent beings, first in their personality, which includes monstrous as well as "heroic" traits;[86] second in nature, with reference to the human and the divine sphere.[87] They partake of both and mediate between the two. This aspect of their nature finds expression in the mixed parentage, human and divine, of type b). This last was the best vehicle for expressing the hero's ambivalent nature, for it is based on a simple and logical model: if human and human produce human, and divine and divine produce divine, a being who partakes of the human and the divine must be the product of a union between human and divine. In category c), the concept of "dubious paternity", in which one version considers the hero as the son of a human father and the other as that of a god, if often blurred with that of double paternity. Thus in Attic legend Theseus was considered the son of Aigeus, but also of Poseidon. I consider the "dubious paternity" motif as primary within a myth over that of "double paternity". This is usually taken for granted, but I think it needs to be argued, especially in view of the fact that, as will be seen, the motif of "double paternity" had a specific mythological value.

Analysis of the motif of "dubious paternity" clearly produces two variant parentages, of type a) and type b). In other words, at the level of form, this motif is a conflation of two such variants **presented as alternatives**. It is reasonable to conclude that stories of dubious paternity emerged in legends which had developed two variants, in one of which the hero's parentage was of type a) and in the other it was of type b). The double paternity motif is a conflation of the variant parentages **by simple juxtaposition**: the two variants are added to each other. This suggests that this motif emerged out of the coexistence, and thus the juxtaposition, of the variants within the same version of the legend. This is the case with the Attic legend of Theseus, in which the coexistence of the two variants was dictated by propaganda considerations. The alternative to this hypothesis is to suppose that the "double paternity" did not emerge through the intermediary of the dubious one and that it did not emerge as a result of the juxtaposition of a) and b) presented as alternatives; but that it was a third primary type of mythological parentage, next to a) and b), created to express something different from either a) or b). This is implausible first at the level of structure: both a) and b) are based on the physiological model "one and one produce one"; the concept of a) plus b) diverges from this model, not to say rejects it. This, I believe, would be surprising in a primary mythological motif. The hypothesis is also implausible at the level of mythological value. The concept of the "double paternity" did not offend the Greek mythological mentality in the way that it offends today's rational thought because it could be absorbed within the concept of the ambivalent nature of the hero and seen as an intensified variant expression of it: not one human parent and one divine, but one human and one divine father at the same time. This is its mythological value. However, there can be no doubt, precisely because it contradicted the physiological model of parentage, that this motif was not a satisfactory vehicle for the expression of this ambivalent nature, in the same way as category b). Hence the subsequent attempts to rationalise the motif by making one paternity real and the other merely putative. This confirms that the motif of double paternity was not created **in order** to express the hero's ambivalent nature, which was anyway best expressed through parentage of type b); and hence also that a) plus b) was not a primary type of parentage, and alternative to a) and b). It must be concluded that the "double paternity" motif emerged as a result of the juxtaposition in the same version of the legend of the alternatives a) and b) and was tolerated because of that ambivalence.

It follows that the appearance of the motif of the dubious or double paternity is best explained as having its ultimate origins in a conflation of two variants of the same legend, one involving two human parents, and one involving one human parent and one divine.

After this motif had become attached to the two major classical heroes, Herakles and Theseus, it could, no doubt, be attracted by imitation to other legends. Hence, I believe, its rare and sporadic appearance in, for example, the legend of Perseus,[88] or in legends of heroes of local importance.

To consider in detail the case of Theseus it will be found that the explanatory model proposed is the one suggested by the historical circumstances of the legend. It is generally believed[89] that Poseidon was Theseus' father in the Troezenian legend, Aigeus in the Attic; and that the problem of the hero's paternity is tied up in the rival claims to be Theseus' homeland of Athens and Troezen, which were eventually harmonised. I consider this to be correct, but intend to test this hypothesis by considering the circumstances of the legend. This study will also throw some additional light, albeit tentatively, on the operation of the mythopeic process and its relation to historical circumstances.

If, as is extremely likely, the saga of Theseus originated in the Mycenaean period,[90] the development of the two local versions can be explained in the following way.

In the early part of the Dark Ages, the pattern of settlement in Greece was one of small, insecure, inward-looking communities. There can be no doubt that this pattern affected the chain of transmission of the Theseus saga. In some places it may have been interrupted and the legend forgotten. Where the legend was preserved, the chain of transmission must have split into many branches which would have developed independently. The distortions of the saga would then be peculiar to each place. Traditions can be distorted, both intentionally and unintentionally, in many ways, and for many reasons.[91] It is certain that, as a secondary element, the **setting** of a tale, which includes the time and place and the names of those involved, is more subject to variation than other elements.[92] Secondary elements can be altered without the essential structure of the original story being affected.[93] Moreover, it is precisely such points that are advantageous to falsify, and corruption in the **setting** has been proved to occur frequently, sometimes because of error and sometimes because of deliberate falsification (n. 92). It is likely then that in t inward-looking communities of the early Dark Ages the localisation of the events of the legend of Theseus was affected by local interests. I believe that this is the context in which emerged the rival claims on Theseus of Attica and Troezen. The story that the hero's father was Aigeus, an Athenian King, is, of cou part of the Athenian claim. It may have been a Mycenaean element, or it may have been invented in the Early Dark Age as part of the process of the localisation of the hero in Attica. Consequently, the story t Poseidon was Theseus' father appears to have a Troezenian origin. This accords well with the fact that, according to one story at least,[94] the amorous encounter between Aithra and Poseidon (whose cult was very important at Troezen) which resulted in the birth of Theseus, took place on Sphairia, an island just off Troezen. In early Attic myth Theseus was the son of mortal parents, a hero of type a). At Troezen, he was of type b).[95]

We must now consider at what period the two variants came into direct contact, and what circumstanc made this contact lead to an attempt at harmonising the two versions. Professor W.G. Forrest suggested to me some time ago that the Kalaureian Amphictyony had probably played an important role in the history of the legend of Theseus. I am convinced that this is correct.

The date of the Amphictyony is controversial,[96] and its discussion is beyond our scope. But I should note that the evidence, such as it is, taken in conjunction with the general situation in the Dark Ages, and the historical circumstances in later centuries, indicates an early date, perhaps in the ninth century, or even in the late tenth.[97] The League was based on the sanctuary of Poseidon at Kalaureia (Poros) off Troezen. Centred on the Saronic Gulf, it had a clearly maritime character; its aims must have been mercantile or military, or both. The fact that, like other early federations, it was based on a sanctuary means that the community of cult provided the model and framework for the federation. Whatever the specific primary purpose of an alliance of this kind, ideological bonds and shared beliefs were important as consolidating elements and focus, and would be developed and promoted. I believe that the legend of Theseus could have been such an element. Since the classical legend combines Troezenian and Athenian elements, one of two things must have happened. Either the saga had developed independently in Ather and Troezen in the early Dark Ages, in which case it constituted a bond between the host city of the Amphictyony and Athens, the member state of the greatest commercial and cultural importance.[98] Or the legend had been localised either at Troezen or at Athens, and was adopted and adapted by the other city at a time in which there were close contacts between Troezen and Athens; such a context can be provided only by the Kalaureian Amphictyony. I consider the latter alternative implausible, for the extant version indicates two chains of transmission which had become differentiated and then gave rise t a compromise version. For example, the two versions of Theseus' paternity, which involve a difference in **nature** and not of personality, are best explained as having arisen in the context of two different local variants. The same is, I think, true of the type of double localisation which appears in the extant legend not a weak association with one area and a strong one with the other, as we may expect if one of the two versions was derivative, but a firm connection with both areas: parts of the legend are firmly set in Troez parts in Attica.

The fact that in one variant Theseus was the son of Poseidon, the main god of the Amphictyony, constituted an additional reason for the promotion of his legend. It appears very likely that the figure and legend of Theseus were indeed promoted in the context of the Kalaureian Amphictyony. Contact between the two variants must surely have led to an attempt at their harmonisation, for while the two rival claims could become divisive, a compromise version, produced and sanctioned by the League, would generate additional bonds within the League, projected into the mythological past, and thus able to legitimate and sanction those of the present. The compromise version had to be based on the creation of legendary connections between Attica and the north-east Peloponnese: its compromise in localisation could be worked out only in terms of movements of the protagonists from one area to the other. And this context best explains why Troezenian elements were accommodated in the myth which formed the basis of the Attic legend of Theseus.

With regard to Theseus' paternity, it was clearly desirable that the compromise legend should include the version in which Theseus was Poseidon's son, and thus of divine and human parentage. But it was also desirable to preserve the figure of the Athenian father, to make sense of, and to confirm the partial localisation of the legend in Attica. The inclusion of both alternatives in the myth resulted in the transformation of the "dubious" or "alternative" paternity into a double paternity which could be tolerated by the Greek mythological mentality. As far as we can tell, attempts at rationalising the double paternity did not take place until after the period here in question, the fifth century.[99]

The harmonisation of the Athenian and Troezenian claims was achieved by the "abandonment" of the pregnant Aithra at Troezen by Aigeus, for which reasons were undoubtedly given in the myth,[100] the subsequent journey of the adolescent Theseus to Athens, and his recognition by Aigeus as his son and heir to the Athenian throne. But this arrangement introduced the motif of the abandonment of a son by his human father, followed by the meeting between father and son when the latter had become a youth. According to the mentality studied in the previous chapter, these circumstances lead to patricide: the initial "hostility" of the (mortal) father towards the son rebounds on the father and provokes his death. Is this relevant here? Need a mythological alteration motivated by strictly non-mythological considerations be moulded by that same mentality?[101] Surely it should. For "mentality" in the sense used here was an ideological pattern of beliefs, in this case about social realities, which determined the "message" of the myth, that is, which provided the mould or one of the moulds in which the mythological material was cast.

As long as those beliefs were held, and those realities remained in being, that mentality should determine the pattern of myths dealing with those problems, whatever the circumstances of their creation. In our case, the abandonment of a baby son by his father should lead to the father's "punishment". But the circumstances of the creation or alteration of a legend determine the precise form of the punishment. In this case the theme of patricide could not be accommodated in the reshaped legend; Theseus could not kill his father in ignorance of his identity. If we judge from the extant legend, the aims and direction of which surely coincide at this point with those of the compromise version, Theseus would have been aware of his father's identity. And Aigeus had to survive so that he might later recognise Theseus as his son and heir, since this recognition and legitimation was important in the transformation of the Troezenian boy to the Athenian hero. Be that as it may, the mentality left its imprint on the legend. Theseus did not commit patricide but he did commit a kind of indirect patricide. His omission to change the sails of his ship led Aigeus to believe that his son had been killed by the Minotaur; in despair, he committed suicide.[102]

This "indirect" patricide appears as a variant of the theme of indirect matricide; not a straight parallel, because Aigeus was *not responsible* for Theseus' *alleged* death (two divergences). Nevertheless, Aigeus' death was the result of Theseus' "hostility by omission". This hostility of son towards father corresponds to the hostility of father towards son inherent in the motif of the abandonment by Aigeus of Theseus, according to the mentality studied in the previous chapter.

The extant legend of Theseus includes another episode involving hostility between the hero and his father: at their first meeting, Aigeus, not realising Theseus' identity, attempted to murder him at the instigation of his wife, Medea. The climax of the episode comes after Aigeus and Medea have put poison in Theseus' drink; just before the hero drinks from his cup, Aigeus sees and recognises the sword which he had left for his son under the rock at Troezen. He thus recognises the unwanted stranger as his son, and proclaims him his heir; Medea is chased out of Attica.

Let us now examine this episode in detail. The tragedies which describe the attempted murder of Theseus by Aigeus and Medea and the subsequent recognition survive in only a few fragments, none of them dealing with the actual poisoning and recognition. Our literary sources give only summaries of the action.

Schol. A *Il.* Λ 741

Μήδεια...φυγὰς εἰς Ἀθήνας ἀφίκετο καὶ ἐγαμήθη
ἐκεῖ Αἰγεῖ τῷ Πανδίονος. κἀκεῖ Θησέα τὸν ἐξ Αἴθρας
γενόμενον τῷ Αἰγεῖ, ἐπὶ τὸν τοῦ πατρὸς ἀναγνωρισμὸν
ἐκ Τροιζῆνος ἀφικόμενον, πείθει τὸν Αἰγέα φάρμακον
αὐτῷ δοῦναι θανάσιμον, ἐπίβουλον αὐτοῦ τῆς βασιλείας
εἰποῦσα παραγίνεσθαι· πεισθεὶς δὲ Αἰγεὺς παραγενο-
μένῳ τῷ παιδὶ φάρμακον ἔδωκεν· μέλλοντος δὲ καταπί-
νειν ἐπιγνοὺς τό τε ξίφος καὶ τὰ ὑποδήματα (ταῦτα
γὰρ ἐν Τροιζῆνι γνωρίσματα κατέλιπεν) τὸ μὲν φάρμακον ἀφείλετο, τὴν δὲ Μήδειαν ἐξέβαλε τῆς Ἀττικῆς.

Plut. *Thes.* xii.2–3

Μήδεια γὰρ ἐκ Κορίνθου φυγοῦσα, φαρμάκοις
ὑποσχομένη τῆς ἀτεκνίας ἀπαλλάξειν Αἰγέα, συνῆν
αὐτῷ. προαισθομένη δὲ περὶ τοῦ Θησέως αὕτη, τοῦ
δὲ Αἰγέως ἀγνοοῦντος, ὄντος δὲ πρεσβυτέρου καὶ
φοβουμένου πάντα διὰ τὴν στάσιν, ἔπεισεν αὐτὸν
ὡς ξένον ἑστιῶντα φαρμάκοις ἀνελεῖν. ἐλθὼν οὖν
ὁ Θησεὺς ἐπὶ τὸ ἄριστον οὐκ ἐδοκίμαζε φράζειν αὐτόν,
ὅστις εἴη, πρότερος, ἐκείνῳ δὲ βουλόμενος ἀρχὴν
ἀνευρέσεως παρασχεῖν, κρεῶν παρακειμένων σπασάμε-
νος τὴν μάχαιραν, ὡς ταύτῃ τέμνων, ἐδείκνυεν ἐκείνῳ.
ταχὺ δὲ καταμαθὼν ὁ Αἰγεύς, τὴν μὲν κύλικα τοῦ
φαρμάκου κατέβαλε, τὸν δὲ υἱὸν ἀνακρίνας ἠσπάζετο,
καὶ συναγαγὼν τοὺς πολίτας ἐγνώριζεν, ἡδέως δεχο-
μένους διὰ τὴν ἀνδραγαθίαν. λέγεται δὲ τῆς κύλικος
πεσούσης ἐκχυθῆναι τὸ φάρμακον ὅπου νῦν ἐν Δελφι-
νίῳ τὸ περίφρακτόν ἐστιν, ἐνταῦθα γὰρ ὁ Αἰγεὺς
ᾤκει, καὶ τὸν Ἑρμῆν τὸν πρὸς ἕω τοῦ ἱεροῦ καλοῦσιν
ἐπ' Αἰγέως πύλαις.

Apollod. i.ix.28

Μήδεια δὲ ἧκεν εἰς Ἀθήνας, κἀκεῖ γαμηθεῖσα
Αἰγεῖ παῖδα γεννᾷ Μῆδον. ἐπιβουλεύουσα δὲ ὕστερον
Θησεῖ φυγὰς ἐξ Ἀθηνῶν μετὰ τοῦ παιδὸς ἐκβάλλεται.

Apollod. *Epit.* i.5–6

Μήδεια δὲ Αἰγεῖ τότε συνοικοῦσα ἐπεβούλευσεν
αὐτῷ. καὶ πείθει τὸν Αἰγέα φυλάττεσθαι ὡς ἐπίβουλον αὐτῷ. Αἰγεὺς δὲ τὸν ἴδιον ἀγνοῶν παῖδα,
δείσας ἔπεμψεν ἐπὶ τὸν Μαραθώνιον ταῦρον. ὡς δὲ
ἀνεῖλεν αὐτόν, παρὰ Μηδείας λαβὼν αὐθήμερον προσήνεγκεν
αὐτῷ φάρμακον. ὁ δὲ μέλλοντος αὐτῷ τοῦ ποτοῦ προσφέρεσ-
θαι ἐδωρήσατο τῷ πατρὶ τὸ ξίφος, ὅπερ ἐπιγνοὺς Αἰγεὺς
τὴν κύλικα ἐξέρριψε τῶν χειρῶν αὐτοῦ. Θησεὺς δὲ
ἀναγνωρισθεὶς τῷ πατρὶ καὶ τὴν ἐπιβουλὴν μαθὼν ἐξέβαλε
τὴν Μήδειαν.

Pausan. ii.iii.8

Μήδεια δὲ τότε μὲν ἐλθοῦσα ἐς Ἀθήνας συνῴ-
κησεν Αἰγεῖ, χρόνῳ δὲ ὕστερον φωραθεῖσα ἐπιβουλεύ-
ειν Θησεῖ καὶ ἐξ Ἀθηνῶν ἔφυγε...

Diod. Sic. iv.55.6

μετὰ δὲ ταῦτα Θησέως ἐπανελθόντος ἐκ Τροιζῆνος
εἰς τὰς Ἀθήνας, ἐγκληθεῖσαν ἐπὶ φαρμακείᾳ φυγεῖν ἐκ
τῆς πόλεως.

Callim. *Hecale* fr. 233 Pfeiffer

ἴσχε τέκος, μὴ πῖθι

(cf. fr. 232: ἡ δ' ἐκόησεν τοὔνεκεν Αἰγέος ἔσκεν).

Dion.Per. 1020–8

Πρὸς δὲ νότον ναίουσιν ἀγινητοὶ ἔθνεα Μήδων,
κείνης τοι γενεῆς ἐρικυδέος ἐκγεγαῶτες
Αἰήταο θυγατρός, ἀμύμονος ἡρωίνης.
εὖτε γὰρ Ἀκταίοιο παρὰ ῥόον Ἰλισσοῖο
φάρμακ' ἐμήσατο λυγρὰ γόνῳ Πανδιονίδαο,
αἰδοῖ μὲν χῶρον κεῖνον λίπεν, ἐς δὲ βαθεῖαν
πλαζομένη κατὰ φῶτας ὁμώνυμον ἵκετο γαῖαν,
οὐ μὲν ἑκὰς Κόλχων· Κόλχων γε μὲν αἶαν ἱκέσθαι
οὔ οἱ ἔην· μῆνιν γὰρ ἑοῦ δειδίσσετο πατρός.

Eustath. Comm. on Dion. Per. 1017.20

αἰδοῖ φησὶ λιποῦσα τὸν Πανδιονίδην Αἰγέα καὶ τὰς
Ἀθήνας, ὅτε λυγρὰ φάρμακα τῷ τοῦ Αἰγέως υἱῷ τῷ
Θησεῖ ἐβουλεύσατο. διὸ φησίν ἀπ' ἐκείνης τῆς Μηδείας,
οἷα σοφῆς φαρμακουργοῦ, ἔτι οἱ Μῆδοι πολυφάρμακοί εἰσι.
τὸ δὲ αἰδοῖ σεμνῶς εἶπεν, οὐ θέλων ἐξυβρίσαι εἰς τὴν
ἡρωΐδα. τῷ ὄντι γὰρ οὐχ ἑκοῦσα ἐκείνη, οὐδὲ δι' αἰδῶ,
ἀλλὰ πρὸς βίαν ἔλιπε τὰς Ἀθήνας, διωχθεῖσα ὑπὸ τοῦ
Αἰγέως, διότι τῷ Αἰγείδῃ Θησεῖ ἐπεβούλευσε κερασαμένη
θανάσιμα φάρμακα, ὁπηνίκα ἐκεῖνος ἐκ Τροιζῆνος χρόνιος
ἐλθὼν μετὰ τοῦ ξίφους καὶ τῶν πεδίλων τῶν πατρικῶν, ἃ
καὶ ὁ Λυκόφρων ἱστορεῖ, ἐνεφανίσθη μὲν ἀγνοοῦντι τῷ
πατρὶ Αἰγεῖ παῖς καλὸς καὶ πρέπων εἰς βασιλείαν, μικροῦ
δὲ ἂν λαθὼν ὑπὸ τῆς Μηδείας ἀπώλετο, εἰ μὴ ὁ πατὴρ
γνωρίσας τὸν ἐκ πολλοῦ ἐπὶ διαδοχῇ τῆς βασιλείας ποθού-
μενον παῖδα περιεσώσατο, καὶ τὸν διαδεξόμενον εὑρηκὼς
ἀπώσατο τὴν Μήδειαν...φασὶ δὲ αὐτὴν δυναστεύσασαν ἐν
Μήδοις...

Ovid. *Met.* vii.404ff.

Iamque aderat Theseus, proles ignara parenti,
et virtute sua bimarem pacaverat Isthmon:
huius in exitium miscet Medea, quod olim
attulerat secum Scythicis aconiton ab oris...

419 .... ea coniugis astu
ipse parens Aegeus nato porrexit ut hosti.
sumpserat ignara Theseus data pocula dextra,
cum pater in capulo gladii cognovit eburno
signa sui generis facinusque excussit ab ore;
effugit illa necem nebulis per carmina motis.
at genitor, quamquam laetatur sospite nato,
adtonitus tamen est ingens discrimine parvo
committi potuisse nefas; fovet ignibus aras
muneribusque deos implet, feriuntque secures
colla torosa boum vinctorum tempora vittis.

Mythogr. Vat. 48

Theseus, Aegei filius et Aethrae, quum a matre sua educatus esset, et ad
puerilem venisset aetatem, petiit Atticam regionem ad cognoscendum patrem...
Medea autem, repudiata ab Iasone, Aegeo nupta persuasit advenientem juvenem
tauro opponere, qui vastabat Atticam regionem, dicens futurum, ut ab eo privaretur
regno. Theseus vero, tauro infecto, duplicavit regi timorem. Dein invitatum ad
epulas eum perdere voluit. Tandem agnito gladio, quem apud Aethram olim
reliquerat, libens agnovit filium, et Medeam, quae fuerat insidiarum causa, pro-
fugere coegit.

Thematically, the first encounter between Theseus and his father is related to averted matricide. In patricide, the hostility originated with the father but the subsequent hostility which leads to the commission of patricide is caused by adverse circumstances, in which the father is no more guilty than the son. In this story, it is the father who initiates the second hostility by attempting to murder his son, as in an "averted matricide". The story diverges from both patricide and averted matricide in one important aspect. Theseus knows that Aigeus is his father, although Aigeus is ignorant of Theseus' identity; therefore Theseus cannot attack Aigeus in anger at the murder plot against him. Moreover it was necessary for the purposes of the legend that Theseus should not kill his father, and that Aigeus should survive to recognise Theseus as his son and heir. Because Aigeus had to survive, the story was modelled on the theme of averted matricide, and not on patricide. Because Theseus was aware of his father's identity, what emerged was a *variant* of averted matricide, with the father in the relevant role.

Some versions show only one attempt at murder, involving the poisoned drink; in others this is preceded by the attempt involving the Marathonian bull. The significance of the second version will be considered in a later chapter. With regard to form, the bull adventure as part of a murder plot is modelled on the motif in which a hero whose death is desired is sent to commit an impossibly difficult, but benevolent, deed; the hero does not die, but comes back victorious, as in the Bellerophon legend.

I shall argue below that the original version of the murder plot against Theseus did not include the bull adventure, and that the attempted poisoning, the primary attempt or at any rate the final one, leads to the recognition. In averted matricide, the attempt fails through a miraculous event which leads to the discovery of the plot. This causes the son to attack the guilty mother with intent to kill, and then chance circumstances lead to recognition and matricide is averted. In this case, since Theseus knew his father's identity, the recognition could only be one-sided. Recognition can avert the murder of the parent or child, as the case may be, only when the attacker is unaware of his/her kinship with the intended victim. Thus in the Theseus story the recognition averts the murder of Theseus by his father, and not, as in averted matricide, the murder of the parent by the son.

Up to this point, the story follows the theme of the averted matricide,[103] transferred to the father and with variations arising from the fact that the legend required that the son be aware of the parent's identity. With this strand is interwoven another, that relating to Medea and to the figure of the stepmother. Medea is in fact presented as the prime mover. Her machinations against Theseus fall into a special category of the wicked stepmother plotting to kill her stepchildren, in which the husband (and father) is ignorant of his son's identity. Consequently, the element of recognition, alien to most "wicked stepmother" plots, halts the murder plan and the conspiracy. A stepmother whose scheming in similar circumstances was successful is Penelope, who persuaded her husband to kill his son Euryalos, of whose identity Odysseus was ignorant. No recognition intervened, and Euryalos was killed.[104]

The pattern of Medea's actions and role is related closely to that of Kreousa's actions and role in Euripides' story of averted matricide (see n. 103 above). Before the recognition, the protagonists there had *imagined* themselves in the following relationships:

Kreousa: Ion's stepmother, but no blood-relation; she attempts to poison him.

Xouthos: Ion's father.

After the recognition, their *real* relationships (of which the audience was aware all along, thanks to the prologue) emerge:

Kreousa: Ion's mother.

Xouthos: her husband, is no blood-relation of Ion's

It is clear that the *false* relationships of the three are symmetrical with the *real* relationships between Theseus, Aigeus and Medea. And the real relationships between Ion, Kreousa and Xouthos appear to be the reversal of their false ones, and thus also the reversal of the relationships between the protagonists in the Theseus legend. Aigeus appears as the reversal of Xouthos: Xouthos believes himself Ion's father, while he is no blood-relation; and Aigeus believes Theseus to be no blood-relation, and tries to kill him, while he is in fact his son. Aigeus is also symmetrical to Kreousa: Kreousa, like Aigeus, thinks her son a stranger, and tries to kill him, as did Aigeus with his son. But in the Theseus story we also have a real stepmother, Medea, who is symmetrical to Kreousa until the recognition between Kreousa and Ion. But Medea is a stepmother, and no recognition altering the course of events refers to a genuine stepmother. It is only in the case of Kreousa, revealed by the recognition to be a mother in stepmother's clothes, that punishment is averted. In other cases in which a stepmother appears in a similar context, she is punished, indeed killed. We know that Medea was punished for having instigated the plot against Theseus, but she was merely exiled from Attica.

Since the plays dealing with these events have been lost, leaving only summaries of the action, whether Medea was attacked and in danger of being killed by Theseus, the injured party, but subsequently saved, is not known. But such an attack would be a natural development on discovery of the murder plot. The attack on the guilty parent is a constant motif of those themes dealing with "hostility of the parent", to which the Theseus story is related. Since Theseus was aware of Aigeus' identity, an attack on Aigeus was excluded. But an attack on the guilty stepmother would make perfect sense both in terms of the plot and in terms of the structure of the related themes discussed in the previous chapter. An attack on Medea would also complete the symmetry between Medea and Kreousa, with only the recognition dislocated and playing a different role because of the different circumstances. It is thus highly plausible that in the extended story Medea was attacked by Theseus. If this is correct, how was her murder averted? What turned her punishment into exile, since no recognition was relevant? I am inclined to see the answer in an external factor. In averted matricide an **external factor** averted the **infanticide**, and the **recognition** averted the **murder of the parent**. There would be a symmetrically reversed situation if where the **recognition** averts the **infanticide**, an **external factor** averted the **murder of the stepmother**. I shall return to this external factor.

The question that demands an answer at this point is when and how this story of the first encounter between Theseus and his father was created and what was its significance in the context of the Theseus legend. The earliest preserved instance of the story is that in Sophocles' or Euripides' *Aigeus*, whichever play is the earlier. I shall return to this. However, it should be noted that Bacchylides' Dithyramb xviii (Snell) can be said to set the stage of the hostility of Aigeus towards Theseus. If this is correct, this dithyramb would presuppose knowledge of the hostile encounter between Theseus and his father.

Some insight into the circumstances of the invention of this story may be gained by considering its position, significance and function within the legend of Theseus. It is clearly a mythological theme in its own right and with its own value, but, like all themes which make up a legend, it also has a role and a function within that legend's structure. From the point of view of the structure of the plot, its function is to provide a tense development to the recognition, which thus comes as a dramatic climax. That is, the theme stresses and emphasises the recognition of Theseus by Aigeus as his son and heir to the Athenian throne. Plutarch (*Thes.* xii.3) tells that after the recognition Aigeus convened the Athenian citizens and presented Theseus to them, recognising him formally; the people received him gladly because of his valour on the road from Troezen to Athens.

The "compromise" version of the legend which reconciled the Troezenian and Athenian claims hinged on two pivots: the "abandonment" of Theseus by his father before he was born, and the subsequent recognition of Theseus as his son and heir by Aigeus. In the extant version the latter has three parts: the *dokimasia* of the lifting of the rock to recover his father's *gnorismata* at Troezen, which resumes Theseus' connection with his Athenian father; the deeds on the road from Troezen to Athens, benevolent actions benefiting the community, belonging to the sphere of the promotion of Theseus into "another Herakles" and representing his transformation from a Troezenian boy into an Athenian hero; and the murder plot and the recognition. It is reasonable to believe that all three are products of the same mythopoeic activity, not only because together they form the second pivot mentioned above and stress the identity of Theseus as an Athenian prince, but also because they are closely interconnected. The *gnorismata*, and especially the sword, provide the means by which Aigeus recognised Theseus and thus halted the murder attempt. The deeds on the road to Athens and the glory of Theseus which follows provide the reason for Aigeus' resentment and fear of Theseus which triggered the murder attempt. The invention of the story about deeds on the road to Athens can be dated, on the evidence of vase-painting: it first appears on vases at about 510. There can be no doubt that this invention belongs in the context of the propaganda activity centred on Theseus associated with the epic *Theseid*.[105] I have argued elsewhere[106] that the episode of the lifting of the rock had also been invented in the late sixth century *Theseid*. This suggests that the same is true of the story of the murder plot. This hypothesis is confirmed by other considerations on the significance of the theme.

Most scholars would agree that the *Theseid*, which promoted the glorification of Theseus as a great Athenian hero, was created under anti-Peisistratid, and specifically Alcmaeonid, influence and inspiration.[107] The emphasis on Theseus' rights to the Athenian throne and the elaboration of his ultimate triumph against evil doers fits better into this late sixth century context, and the aspirations of Kleisthenes, who was presented as Theseus' historical counterpart, than into any other context of mythopoeic activity. Indeed, I shall go further. I suggest that the theme of the murder plot as a whole is a mythological counterpart to the achievements, or the aspirations depending on the exact date of the composition of the *Theseid* (but see n. 108 below), of the anti-Peisistratid, and specifically the Alcmaeonid, party. It represents Theseus, Kleisthenes' mythological counterpart, coming from outside Athens, although Athenian, as did Kleisthenes and the Alcmaeonids, to be treated with hostility as a potential usurper and revealed ultimately as the legitimate heir to the Athenian throne. If Aigeus is taken as representing the Athenian people, and the wicked stepmother the Peisistratids, the parallel is complete. Aigeus, misled by his wicked wife, tried to kill Theseus, whom he considered a potential usurper while in fact he was his son and legitimate heir. Similarly the Athenian people, misled by the tyrants, did not support the Leipsydrion attempt, which thus resulted in failure and massacre. But in the end, as in the case of Theseus, justice triumphed and the tyrants were chased away, as had Theseus' stepmother been,[108] and a legitimate (that is, democratic) leadership with the interests of the Athenian people at heart was established. The correspondence between myth and history is too close to be due to coincidence, but must deliberately have been contrived. It must have been shaped in such a way that its pattern corresponded to that of an embellished version of the historical events, so that it became their mythological prefiguration.

It is not difficult to reconstruct the process of its creation. The mind of a Greek creating a myth who approached the episode of the first encounter between Theseus and his father and who wanted to invent an interesting development to the climax of the recognition that he intended to stress would naturally conjure up the motif of parent-child hostility. In Greek myth the first encounter between a grown-up son and a parent who had abandoned him leads automatically to a parent-child hostility. In this case, it could not result in patricide. Once he had thought out the motif, given the identification of Theseus with Kleisthenes, the possibility of making it the mythological prefiguration of the historical events, or rather of a biased version of them, must have become apparent. Hence the creation of this theme in this particular form. The theme could not have been presented explicitly in the poem as the mythological prefiguration of the expulsion of the tyrants. But the reader or listener would naturally have associated the two thematic patterns and make the connection, given his awareness of the equivalence Theseus = Kleisthenes, and the aim and direction of the whole poem, the glorification of Theseus as a great Athenian and anti-Peisistratid hero.

Theseus' reception by his divine father and his divine stepmother at the bottom of the sea is first found on vases in the last quarter of the sixth century.[109] Its earliest surviving instance in literature is in Bacchylides'

Dithyramb xvii (Snell), probably of the 470s. It is generally believed[110] that this theme was created in correspondence to Herakles' introduction to Olympus as a result of the fact that the legend of Theseus came to be modelled in general on that of Herakles. But the correspondence is not precise. Herakles' introduction to Olympus is his apotheosis, after his death: Herakles came to stay at Olympus. Theseus' reception at the bottom of the sea signifies his recognition as son of Poseidon during his lifetime. The basic significance of the themes is the same, but the considerable divergence in form indicates that if Herakles' introduction to Olympus was the stimulus for the creation of this motif at this level of significance, its form was based on another model, which I believe to be the theme of the first reception of Theseus by his mortal father and stepmother. The themes are related, but in a way reversed. The mortal father and stepmother received Theseus with hostility and tried to murder him; the divine ones received him with love and offered him their protection. Whether the latter motif was also treated in the *Theseid* or was created in the years immediately after the epic's composition, I believe that its form was inspired by the theme of the first encounter between Theseus, Aigeus and Aigeus' wife. It is fitting that the two "recognitions" of Theseus, as the son of Aigeus and heir to the Athenian throne and as the son of a god, should be related in thematic structure.

It is interesting to note that the theme of Theseus at the bottom of the sea presents the hero as more privileged than Herakles in his dealings with his divine relatives. During his lifetime Herakles had suffered the intense hostility of his divine stepmother.

To sum up. The legend of Theseus does not include the motif of hostility to the mother. Hostility between parent and child does appear, but is referred to the father. Aigeus dies by a type of indirect patricide. He had attempted to murder Theseus, as mothers do in similar circumstances. However, it was not he, but his wife, Theseus' stepmother, who attracted the hero's answering hostility.

5. The iconographical motif of a youth attacking a woman with a sword

Since the possibility of Theseus' attacking his mother Aithra with murderous intent has been excluded, how might the fact that on Makron's cup the protagonists were labelled "Theseus" and "Aithra" by the vase-painter be explained? The simple explanation was first suggested *en passant* by Smith[111] but did not attract any attention. His idea is simply that mother and stepmother, Aithra and Medea, have been confused on the inscribed Makron cup. In other words, Makron made a mistake in the inscriptions. This would be neither rare nor surprising. Another such example of a confusion in a Theseus scene springs to mind: a fragment of a lekanis in Leningrad mentioned in CB ii, 81, on which a youth with chlamys and spears is pursuing a woman; the youth is inscribed "Theseus", the woman "Thetis". As Caskey and Beazley remark, it cannot be doubted that the woman's inscribed name is the result of a slip, caused by confusion with pictures of Thetis pursued by Peleus. The most reasonable explanation of the peculiarity of the *dramatis personae* of Makron's cup is that they are the result of just such a confusion.

That slip of the vase-painter's brush is very plausible and easy to understand in the framework of the rules governing such slips. Fromkin[112] has studied slips of the tongue with the aim of illustrating the mechanism of speech they reveal and has thrown some light on the mental grammar of linguistic communication and on the mechanics of errors of speech. Her conclusions seem as valid for slips of the pen as for slips of the tongue, since, not surprisingly, it is at the level of linguistic encoding that "noise", or interference, appears to produce errors of speech.[113] It is irrelevant that in the case of slips of the pen the neural signals would be sent to the hand rather than to the vocal area. Slips of the tongue and slips of the pen are non-random and predictable; one can predict the *kinds* of error that will occur, since they are conditioned by the mechanics of word selection, the organisation of the mental dictionary, and by mental grammar in general. The replacement of "Medea" by "Aithra" is a "predictable" slip in the sense that it is the kind of slip that we can expect given the way in which linguistic encoding is carried out.

Fromkin has argued convincingly that[114] "the semantic representation of a word is a composite of hierarchically ordered semantic features". In errors of speech the correct and substituted word are thus often seen to fall into the same semantic class, as in "blond eyes" for "blond hair" and "my boss's husband" for "my boss's wife". In the case in question, the correct word "Medea" and the substituted "Aithra" clearly belong to the same semantic category when the referent is Theseus. Moreover, "Aithra" can be considered the opposite of "Medea" (again with reference to Theseus) since in one sense "stepmother" and "mother" are opposites. In speech errors, we find that the correct word may be replaced by its antonym: "like" for "hate", "big" for "small", and so on. There is clearly no difficulty from the point of view of the mechanics of mental slips in considering "Aithra" a mental slip/slip of the pen for "Medea". The circumstances of this case would be particularly propitious for replacing the name of the stepmother with that of the mother, since there was an additional parameter encouraging such a scrambling: the subject of "averted stepmatricide" of the scene would evoke in the mind of an early fifth century Athenian the related concept of "averted matricide" with which it forms a mythological and hence (when operating at the mythological level) mental recall-nexus. The two concepts would be in the vase-painter's mind at the time when word selection was taking place, encouraging "noise" or "interference" in the act of communication in general.[115]

The *psychological* causes of such slips are a different matter, and in a way, irrelevant: whatever psychological factors may have lain behind Makron's switch from "mother" to "stepmother" — and it would be very easy, though idle, to speculate — what I am concerned with is showing that the slip was possible and indeed plausible in terms of mental grammar, word-selection and mechanics of mental slips.

As for the mechanics of this particular error in word selection, it could have taken place in two ways.[116] The first is to suppose that the slip happened through simple underspecification, which can produce striking slips in the process of word selection. Fromkin[117] quotes the substitution of "dachshund" for "Volkswagen" and explains it through underspecification: the person seems to have selected a word which matched the semantic features "small, German". In our case the underspecification would not have been so extreme. Makron would have selected a word (Aithra) to match the semantic features "female, in parental relationship to Theseus" instead of "female, in parental relationship to Theseus through marriage to his father, no blood relation" – or whatever the mental sentence expressing these concepts would have been. The second model is to suppose that the specification had been correct, but that the antonym, insofar as we can consider "Aithra" the antonym of "Medea" as seen above, was substituted.

The slip once made, it would not of necessity follow that the painter would detect it and correct it before the red pigment dried, any more than we can always detect our own slips of the pen or of the typewriter.[118] Finally, it is possible that we are not dealing with a slip of the pen/brush at all, but with a slip of the tongue. We cannot be absolutely certain, although it appears likely, that the inscriptions were written by the vase-painter himself. It is conceivable that the substitution "Aithra" for "Medea" may have been an original slip of the *tongue* by Makron while giving directions to the inscription writer.

The possibility that Aithra was correctly named and Theseus' name a slip can be excluded. The youth is portrayed, here and in the other scenes of the series, according to the canonical iconography of Theseus; and the iconographical motif was too popular to have shown an unknown attack on Aithra. With regard to the known stories in the context of which an attack could have taken place, though no such privileged treatment would have been warranted, we can note the following.

Perhaps the only youths likely to have attacked Aithra are the Dioscuri, who took her prisoner when they freed Helen who had been abducted by Theseus. But Aithra was by then old, while on Makron's cup and in other scenes of the series the woman is young; there is no reason to believe that the Dioscuri had reason physically to attack Aithra with a sword and to imperil her life; and two Dioscuri rather than one may have been expected. Another theoretical possibility is that someone may have attacked Aithra in the confusion during the Sack of Troy. There are scenes showing Aithra in the course of the Sack of Troy, being rescued by her grandsons Demophon and Akamas, and she is always represented as an old woman.

The woman Theseus is shown attacking with a sword must surely be Medea. Indeed there is no other woman whom Theseus would have reason or occasion to attack with murderous intent. Now, however, we must consider whether there are iconographical arguments in favour of, or against, the hypothesis that the scenes represent Theseus attacking Medea. But before considering the iconography, the scenes dealing with events after Theseus' arrival in Athens should be examined, and the iconography of Medea, and of other characters involved, studied to form an iconographical foundation on which the study can be based.

Among the events after Theseus' arrival in Athens[119] the following are shown in art:
1. The capture of the bull of Marathon.
2. Medea persuading Aigeus to poison Theseus.
3. The attempted poisoning.
4. The recognition.[120]

The first episode has been studied by Shefton, and I shall consider it last and in some detail.

The second episode is on the following monuments:

i. Attic red-figured skyphos Florence P 80 (Webster/Trendall III.3.2). On one side of the vase is the bull, tied to a tree; on the other, Medea, in oriental dress and holding the box of poisons, approaches the seated Aigeus, who holds a sceptre.

ii. (The conspiracy perhaps less explicit). A crowded scene, including the already defeated bull, on a krater at Adolphseck by the Kekrops Painter (ARV^2 1346,2; Brommer, *Schl. Fasan.* fig. 21). Medea, wearing oriental dress and holding a jug and phiale, leans against Aigeus' throne.

iii. Red-figured skyphos from Spina, Ferrara T.238C (Alfieri, *Mél. Piganiol* ii, 615 fig. 2). Side A shows Theseus and the bull. On side B, Aigeus, with black hair, beard and sceptre, is seated; Medea in oriental dress, proffers to him a half-open box; between them, a thymiaterion.

The third episode is on the following:

i. In a series of Roman terracotta reliefs (Rohden/Winnefeld 100–2, figs. 187–8, pls. lii, cix; *AA* 1912, 128 fig. 20; Breitenstein nos. 863–4, pl. 112; *MuM* 18 [1958] no. 72). A list of all such reliefs showing the attempted poisoning can be found in Brommer, *Denkmälerlisten* ii, 4–5. A fragmentary marble version of these terracotta reliefs is illustrated in *BdI* 1867, 199). Most of these reliefs show Theseus seated, wearing sandals, sword hanging at his flank. Aigeus, bearded, stands before him and leans towards the hero, urging him to drink from a phiale which he proffers. Medea stands rigid behind Aigeus, in chiton and himation. Aigeus' body partly hides her. Some reliefs show an enlarged version in which Theseus, Aigeus and Medea are flanked on each side by a female spectator; see the relief British Museum D 607 (Walters *BM Catal.* 402, where the scene is interpreted as the healing of Machaon by Nestor); Rohden/Winnefeld 101 fig. 187, and commentary 101–2. In my opinion the style of the reliefs recalls that of Attic sculpture of the third quarter of the fifth century. It cannot be excluded that they may reflect an original of that date.

ii. On an Early Neoattic tripod base from the Athenian Agora (Brommer, *Denkmälerlisten* 5; Harrison, *Agora* xi, 79–81, no. 128 pl. 30). There are three archaistic figures, one on each side of the base: a youth with cloak and club, a king with a sceptre, and a woman with a phiale. Harrison very plausibly identifies them as Theseus, Aigeus and Medea. Aigeus faces Theseus, while Medea approaches the youth from the other side; her left hand, which is missing, was raised, and she may have been holding an oinochoe. Harrison seems to suggest that the context is that of the struggle with the bull. But the precise moment within that general area of the Theseus cycle is not the struggle with the bull but its aftermath, the attempted poisoning of Theseus by Aigeus and Medea. The bull is not shown, and Theseus is represented resting and standing between Aigeus and Medea, both of whom turn towards him. Medea is busy with her phiale, and perhaps jug, while approaching Theseus. All these iconographical elements indicate that the poison attempt is depicted. Harrison[121] thinks that "the presence of the hero with the club suggests that we have a reference to the content of a choral composition, presumably a dithyramb, sung by the tribe that won the tripod".

I know of only one scene in Greek art which depicts the fourth episode, the recognition; that on the Apulian bell-krater Schloss Fasanerie 179 by the Adolphseck Painter (Cambitoglou/Trendall 19–20, no. 1; Webster/Trendall III.3,3; *CVA* pl. 80.1–2).[122] Theseus, in the middle, leans on his club and pours a libation on an altar; he wears a cloak and petasos. On the other side of the altar stands Aigeus, a sceptre resting on his elbow, examining Theseus' sword, one of the *gnorismata* he himself had hidden under the rock at Troezen, and holding Theseus' pilos. Medea, to the left of Theseus, in heavily patterned peplos and shawl, expresses so much astonishment and terror at the recognition that she has dropped the jug which she had used to pour the poisoned drink into Theseus' phiale. This scene, which represents "a very Attic" subject on a South Italian vase, has convincingly been connected with the performance of an Athenian play.[123]

The subject of the recognition is also once found in the repertory of non-Greek art under Greek influence, in a group of silver vessels, going under the name of "Bactrian bowls",[124] probably produced in Hellenized Bactria and at least to some extent related to the so-called "Megarian bowls". Of all the interpretative hypotheses suggested for the scenes they carry,[125] the most convincing seems that put forward by Weitzman[126] and accepted by Denwood:[127] that they reflect themes from the Greek literary tradition, which had spread to the East through Alexander's conquests and the Hellenistic kingdoms. Weitzman has interpreted many of the motifs as illustrating scenes from Euripidean tragedies. Among them he thinks he can detect an illustration from the *Aigeus* showing the recognition scene on the New York bowl (Weitzman 317–8; figs. 13; 23). Only one figure, Aigeus, from the recognition scene is said to be depicted, in the figure of an old, bearded man holding a jug in his raised left hand, and an empty kylix, the bowl turned frontally towards the spectator, in his right. Weitzman admits that the omission of both Theseus and Medea is awkward, but believes that he can remedy this by imagining that the figure next to Aigeus, whom he interprets as Theseus scolding Hippolytos over the matter of Phaedra, also belongs in part to the recognition scene. He suggests that the two scenes involving Theseus have been combined, with the one figure of Theseus functioning in both scenes. It seems to me, however, that there is a much simpler, and iconographically coherent, explanation. If the Hippolytos theme is eliminated and all three figures taken together, they would belong to a scene showing the recognition of Theseus by Aigeus and the defeat of Medea. Let us consider the figures: Theseus is seated, leaning on the hilt of his sword which is in its scabbard, and which is given a very prominent place in the picture. His right hand is raised, index and middle fingers pointing at the figure standing in front of him. This figure is not so clearly a man as Weitzman seems to believe, but on the contrary looks very much like two other figures on the same bowl which Weitzman identifies as female: fig. 14; "Megara" and fig. 16: "the daughter of Pelias". It is also very different from the male figures. The fact that the breasts are not clearly shown is due to the stance: this figure has folded and crossed her arms over her breasts, left hand open, palm upwards, in a gesture of entreaty. The averted head expresses shame, real or feigned, which Medea had every reason to feel, or to pretend she felt, while Hippolytos had none. Generally, the stance is most unsuitable for a young and virile huntsman like Hippolytos, but very suitable for a woman, especially one full of guile like Medea. The other way in which the figure differs from other female figures is the dress. In this, however, she differs from all other figures, male and female, on this or any other bowl of this type that I have seen. Weitzman[128] describes the garment as "a tunic with long sleeves and wide trousers, similar to those worn by Persian hunters on works of Sassanian art". To me, this garment looks like an adapted version of the "Oriental costume" of Greek iconography, of the type worn for example, by some Amazons. In the same way, the peplos and the himation of the other figures are adaptations of the peplos and the himation proper. But here the adaptation was carried further, since this was a dress inspired by Oriental models which would have been available to influence the adaptation of their Greek version. This peculiarly oriental type of dress, amid garments inspired from classical Greek ones, suggests that in the model or models the bowl was copying or adapting — or if the model was literary, which inspired it — the figure standing in front of Theseus was dressed in oriental costume. While Hippolytos had no reason thus to be depicted, Medea is one of the two people with whom Theseus was involved who did. The other was his Amazon wife. If all three figures are taken together, and interpreted as Aigeus, Theseus and Medea just after the recognition, the scene would make better sense iconographically; moreover, the awkwardness of Aigeus' isolation and Theseus' double role would disappear.[129]

Let us consider now the first of the four episodes listed above, that of Theseus and the bull. The scenes representing Theseus struggling with the Marathonian bull have been discussed in detail by Shefton,[13] who argues that the woman in Greek dress holding a phiale and jug who is present in some of the scenes is not Medea, but a local nymph who was on the side of the bull and made a libation for the beast's victory. It is necessary for our purposes to consider this problem more closely since it affects vitally the iconography of Medea.

Shefton's argument is as follows. The woman with the phiale and jug is not Medea because "there is nothing specific to point to a Medea".[131] By this he means mainly, and this becomes explicit in the course of his discussion, that she is not wearing oriental costume. I shall discuss in some detail the problem of oriental costume, but first two points should be made. First, Medea has no particular attribute which characterises her elsewhere and is missing here; the box of poisons appears only in some rather late scenes. Her identity is normally indicated through the context and her role in the action.[132] Second, there is indeed "something" which characterises her as Medea in the scenes with the struggle of Theseus against the bull: the phiale and jug which she will use for the preparation and serving of the poison in the second murderous attempt against Theseus. She is holding, or rather dropping, the jug in the Apulian scene with the recognition of Theseus, and the phiale, and perhaps also the jug, on the Neoattic base with the poison attempt. Although Shefton sees the logic of this, and that the phiale and jug would fit Medea admirably, he dismisses this interpretation; he opts instead for the *lectio difficilior* of a local nymph making a libation in support of the bull. But there is an objection to this which, in my opinion, invalidates Shefton's theory: the *Lokalpersonifikation* of Marathon, where the struggle with the bull took place, was not a nymph but the eponymous hero of the deme of Marathon, *Marathon,* who, like Theseus, Athena and Heracles, was shown in the representation of the battle of Marathon in the Stoa Poikile.[133]

Shefton argued that the woman present in the bull struggle is Medea only if she wears oriental dress. The assumption is that Medea is always represented dressed in oriental costume, which is incorrect. Simon has criticised this assumption[134] and remarks that it is only in the second half of the fifth century that Medea is given the barbarian, oriental dress[135] and even then it does not become obligatory. In black-figure, Medea does not wear oriental dress: see, for instance, the neck-amphora London B 221 (*ABV* 321,4), and the hydria London B 328 (*ABV* 363,42), both showing Medea and the Peliads. Medea also wears Greek dress on some red-figured vases, and especially on the earlier ones. See the following examples: hydria London E 163 (*ARV*^{2} 258,26) by the Copenhagen Painter (second quarter of the fifth century); the identification of Medea here is doubly certain, indicated both by the context and by inscriptions; stamnos Berlin 2188 (*ARV*^{2} 297,1) by the Hephaisteion Painter (first quarter of the fifth century); cup Bologna PU 273 (*ARV*^{2} 1268,1) by the Kodros Painter (third quarter of the fifth century); this is probably a genre scene which has been elevated to the mythological level through the inscriptions, a not infrequent phenomenon in Greek vase-painting. Medea also wears Greek dress on the terracotta reliefs with the poison attempt discussed above, for which a fifth century original cannot be excluded, and on some South Italian vases, including the krater with the recognition scene.[136]

The basis of the argument against recognising the woman as Medea is thus incorrect. Let us nevertheless consider its other aspects, so that no lingering doubt can remain.

An obvious argument for the idea that the woman in Greek dress is indeed Medea lies, as Shefton saw, in the fact that the undisputed, orientally dressed, Medea carries the same phiale and jug as the alleged nymph in some bull scenes. The natural explanation would be that the two sets belong together, with Medea in both, and that in some later scenes Medea has been given oriental costume. But Shefton has again adopted the *lectio difficilior*: he sees a break in the iconographical tradition, consisting of the displacement of the nymph by Medea, with the latter also taking over the "nymph's" phiale and jug. Apart from the inherent improbability of any such process, this hypothesis also leaves unexplained why, if Medea acquired the phiale and jug in the bull-scenes only through a takeover from the nymph she replaces, the phiale, or the phiale and the jug, should be associated with the poison attempt and the recognition scene in the monuments we have considered above. It is too much to seek a coincidence. The solution is simple: the phiale and jug belong to the iconographical type of Medea in the context of the poison attempt, to be used for preparing and serving the poison. In the bull scenes the phiale and jug hint at the second, and last, attempt to murder Theseus after the bull's failure, in the same way that Medea's presence in the bull scenes hints at the fact that she was the instigator of the plot. Shefton has objected that if the woman in Greek dress were Medea,[137] we should have to explain why she should still be wearing Greek dress on two vases painted within the period in which Medea regularly wears oriental costume in

Attic iconography.[138] The explanation is again simple: an established iconographical pattern, like that of Theseus and the bull, need not necessarily have been altered to include fashionable innovations. Some vase-painters may have wished to bring Medea's dress up to date, and others may not. There is indeed a parallel of at least one case in which Medea has maintained the Greek dress in a scene with an established iconographical pattern within the period in which she is normally given oriental dress: in the representation of Medea, the Peliads and the ram, and Medea and Pelias, on an unattributed cup in the Vatican of the last quarter of the fifth century (*AZ* iv [1846] pl. xl; Séchan, *Tragédie* 478 fig. 136; Lambrinoudakis pl. 8).

There are also ramifications of the main line of Shefton's argument which do not convince. On the bell-krater in Madrid red 217, by the Painter of Munich 2335 (*ARV*^{2} 1163,45), two women are present at the struggle of Theseus with the bull; Medea, in oriental dress and holding the phiale (the hand which would have held the jug is hidden behind the bull), and another woman, only the upper part of whose body is shown (which may, but need not, mean that she is emerging from the ground), and who wears a stephane and raises her hand. As Shefton remarks, she is taking the side of Theseus. He takes her to be that local nymph, who elsewhere would have been replaced by Medea. Here the nymph is also present but Medea is holding on to the phiale which she took over from the nymph who, on this occasion, has changed sides. This complex process of part-substitution is rather unlikely, and we have seen that the *Lokalpersonifikation* of Marathon was the hero Marathon and not a local nymph. We can add, in iconographical argument, that the "nymph" here is a matronly figure, while in the other scenes the woman holding phiale and jug is youthful. The woman on the Madrid krater, whether or not she is emerging from the ground, could satisfactorily be explained as a divinity, Hera or Gaia, for example, watching the fight, in a way that may partly recall the divinities shown as spectators at the fight with the bull which has just ended on the krater Adolphseck, Schloss Fasanerie 78 by the Kekrops Painter (*ARV*^{2} 1346,2) mentioned above.

I hope that I have shown that the iconographical case and the iconographical arguments against recognising Medea in the woman with the Greek dress, phiale and jug, are anything but strong. Let us now examine Shefton's overall conclusions, and the way in which he relates the iconographical to the literary evidence: "... before about 430 B.C. there is no pictorial evidence that Medea played any part in the story of Theseus' encounter with the bull. We should not, of course, expect to find her in any representation of the canonical version of the myth ... and indeed in the fifth century vase-pictures assembled on p. 159 (nos. 1–6), we find a nymph on the very place we might have expected Medea, had she been about. From about 430 onwards, however, we have seen that there is substantial evidence for the currency of what we called the 'variant' version of the legend. It is quite likely that it was Euripides' *Aigeus* which gave it its currency, and we must note that the vase-pictures which first reflect this 'variant' version and show the presence of Medea fall outside the iconographic tradition of the theme as though they had been attracted out of their orbit by some powerful new influence". Thus two hypotheses, literary and iconographical, are made, by circular, if implicit, argument, to support each other and to provide mutual confirmation. We have seen that the iconographical hypothesis is implausible; let us examine the literary evidence. To begin with, it is merely an assumption that Euripides invented, or was the first to present in tragic form, the version of the myth in which Medea is responsible for Theseus' struggle with the bull, as opposed to its being a voluntary benevolent deed of Theseus. Indeed, Pearson has argued most convincingly[140] that in Sophocles' *Aigeus* — the date of which is not known, but which could be earlier than Euripides' play — the struggle with the bull and its capture also preceded the poison attempt and the recognition. But let us suppose for a moment that Euripides did indeed invent the so-called variant; since the date of his *Aigeus* is not known, indeed to provide a date for it is part of Shefton's case, then the alleged iconographical "break" can be significant only if it is made to date the play. If an earlier date is given to the play, the mirage break, even if it existed (which is not the case) would have no relevance to the play, or the play to it. In fact, Webster,[141] who also attributes the "variant" version to Euripides, dates the play much earlier because he argues that Shefton's "nymph" is none other than Medea. He agrees with Page[142] that the fashion of dressing Medea in oriental dress was started by Euripides' *Medea* in 431, and thinks that from then onwards artists could give Medea oriental or Greek dress at will.

It seems that there is every justification to conclude that the woman, sometimes in Greek dress, sometimes in oriental, holding a phiale and a jug in the scenes depicting the struggle between Theseus and the bull is Medea.

Consideration of the scenes representing events which took place in Athens after the arrival of Theseus indicate (apart from Theseus, whose iconography does not differ from the regular Theseus iconography) that Aigeus is represented as a bearded old king with a sceptre; and that Medea can wear Greek or oriental dress. Her role in the poison attempt is indicated by her holding the phiale and jug, or the jug alone if Theseus has already taken the phiale with the poison, as in the scene of the recognition on the Apulian krater. On this same krater, the scene takes place next to an altar.

We should now turn to the original problem, the group of scenes with a youth attacking a woman with a sword, and to their iconography, to consider whether they can offer evidence towards the woman's identification; and in particular, whether they confirm or invalidate the suggestion that she is Medea, and that the scene represents Theseus' attack on her after the poison attempt was discovered.

I list and describe briefly the scenes:

1. Cup Leningrad 649 (St. 830) by Makron (ARV^2 460,13; Dugas/Flacelière pl. 10; Pfuhl, *MuZ* fig. 445; here **pl. 1a**).

This scene has already been discussed in great detail.

2. Oinochoe Boston 03.786 by Myson (ARV^2 242,80; unpublished)

To the left a youth, wearing a chiton, himation thrown over his left shoulder and upper arm, and without petasos, moves to the right, about to attack a woman, sword in hand; his left arm, stretched forward, disappears behind the woman who flees to the right, her head turned back towards the youth, her right arm extended towards him in a gesture of supplication. Next to her, another woman flees to the right and turns back towards the scene; her right arm is raised in dismay and shock, her left pulls her himation in the stock gesture of fleeing maidens.

I consider this a late work of Myson. Mrs Louise Berge, whose doctoral thesis was dedicated to Myson, has kindly permitted me to mention that she agrees with me about the date of this vase, which should be placed between *ca* 480 and 475.

3. Lekythos Oxford 1920.103 by the Providence Painter (ARV^2 640,71; *CVA* pl. 38,8; here **pl. 1b**).

The youth advances against the woman, drawn sword in his right hand, left arm extended in front of him, holding the scabbard. The woman turns as she flees and makes a gesture of supplication with her right hand. Beazley (*CVA* op.cit.) dated this lekythos to about 480. The high date is the consequence of the fact that at that time Beazley was dating the Providence Painter earlier than he did subsequently. This date should be brought down and there is nothing in the vase that need be earlier than the 460s. In 1954 Beazley dated the lekythos Boston 95.44, also by the Providence Painter (ARV^2 640,76; 1663; Ghali-Kahil, *Enlèv.* pl. 85.1) "about 470–460" (CB ii,43). This Boston lekythos looks earlier than Oxford 1920.103 and a date in the 460s is the most likely one for the Oxford lekythos.

4. Astarita cup in the Vatican by the Penthesilea Painter (ARV^2 880,13; see CB ii,63 n. 2; unpublished).

On the fragmentary tondo an altar is shown to the right, to which the woman flees, pursued by the youth, who holds a drawn sword, scabbard hanging at his side. The woman's arms, hands open, palms turned upwards in supplication, are extended both toward the altar where she seeks sanctuary, and toward the youth. A club and a pilos at the left corner rest against the circumference of the tondo. They underline the youth's identity: Theseus.

5. Pelike Manchester iii.I.41 by Hermonax (ARV^2 486,42; *AJA* 49 [1945] 497 fig. 12; see also Webster, *Memoirs Manchester* 87 [1946–7] 6; here **pl. 2a**).

The youth has a petasos thrown at the back of his neck, and scabbard hanging at his side; the sword is in his right hand, his left arm is extended toward the woman. She is fleeing and looking back, left arm forwards, palm upwards.

6. Nolan amphora in the collection of Cologne University, by Hermonax (ARV^2 488,78; unpublished. I was able to consult photographs very kindly provided by Dr Eberhard Thomas of the Archäologisches Institut der Universität zu Köln).

On side A a youth, petasos thrown at the back of his neck, naked but for a wrap thrown over his extended left arm and falling behind his back, advances towards a fleeing woman shown on side B. He has a sword in his right hand, and holds the scabbard in his left. The woman on B turns to look at the aggressor as she flees.

7. Hydria fragment Oxford 1966.508 by an undetermined Mannerist, recalling the Leningrad Painter (ARV^2 587,55; *Paralipomena* 393,55; *Beazley Gifts* pl. xxv.221; here **pl. 2b**).

It is listed, both in ARV^2 and in *Beazley Gifts* as "an unexplained subject". The description in the latter reads: "on the left, 1, youth in chlamys and pilos striding to right, looking back as he sheaths or unsheaths his sword, 2, a woman in a chiton rushing to right". There is no reason for dissociating this scene from the series showing a youth attacking a woman with a sword.[143] The youth in this series does sometimes have a pilos instead of petasos, and can wear the chlamys. The only difference is that the actual attack is not in process but is about to begin or has just finished. In the latter case, which in view of the fact that youth and woman seem to be moving in opposite directions may be more likely, the woman would be escaping with her life; this would fit Medea admirably, since she was not killed but exiled in punishment for her attempted murder.

8. Stamnos in the British Museum, London E 446 by the Painter of the Yale oinochoe (ARV^2 502,4; *CVA* pl. 22.1; here **pl. 3a**).

While in most scenes the woman is fleeing to the right (of the spectator), here the movement is to the left. And two additional figures frame the main scene. The youth, sword in his right hand, grabs the woman by the hair with his left; she makes a gesture of supplication with her left hand. It should be noted that "grasping by the hair" is an iconographical motif indicating violence, normally preliminary to killing. To the right, a woman spectator raises her hand in alarm. To the left, a bearded man with a sceptre also raises his hand in alarm. With regard to the significance of the scene, the ARV^2 caption reads: "youth with a sword pursuing a woman (Theseus and Aithra?)". Walters, in *CVA*, interprets the scene as the killing of Klytaimestra in the presence of Aegisthus and Elektra. But there are many difficult involved in such an interpretation. First, in the representational evidence of the vases, the killing of Aegis precedes that of Klytaimestra. Second, the bearded king on our scene does not in any way behave as thou he were intimately involved in the action, as, for instance, a prospective victim, but as an interested, alarme spectator. He cannot be Aegisthus. Third, the female spectator is, as Walters acknowledged, making a startled gesture. If she were Elektra, she would be making a gesture of encouragement, as indeed she does in the scenes in which she does appear. In these circumstances, it seems that the suggestion that the scene represents the death of Klytaimestra is fallacious. If the scene is considered to belong to the series interpreted as showing Theseus attacking Medea, the iconographical pattern can satisfactorily be explained: the king would be Aigeus, the third participant in the episode of attempted poisoning and recognition. The presence of the woman at the other side may have been determined by the desire to balance the composition by framing the two main figures. A startled woman spectator at a scene of violence is a stock iconographical motif added at will.

9.   Bell-krater Leningrad 777 (St. 1786) by the Painter of the Yale oinochoe (ARV^2 502,11; Peredolskaya pl. cxvi).

The woman turns back to look at her pursuer as she flees and makes a gesture of supplication with her right hand (hand open, palm upwards).

10.   Neck amphora New York 41.162.155 by the Painter of the Yale oinochoe (ARV^2 502,14; *CVA* Gallatin pl. 18.2,4).

The youth is naked but for a cloak thrown over his left arm, which is extended forward; he holds the scabbard in his left hand, the sword in his right. The woman turns while fleeing and makes a frightened gesture.

11.   Cup Louvre C 10932 by the Sabouroff Painter (ARV^2 837,6; unpublished).

An early work of the artist. The movement in the tondo scene is from right to left, which is unusual, but not unique in the series. The youth wears chiton, cloak and pilos, and moves from right to left, sword in his right hand, left arm covered by the cloak and extended forward toward the woman who flees to the left and turns to look at her aggressor.

12.   Pelike at Charlecote, Fairfax-Lucy Collection, by the Agrigento Painter (ARV^2 578,68; hitherto unpublished. I am very grateful to Mr O.J. Pattison for allowing me to publish the photograph, pl. 3b. The photograph was taken by Professor John Boardman.)

A youth, naked but for a cloak thrown over his upper arm, petasos thrown at the back of his neck, advances toward a woman, drawn sword in his right hand, scabbard in his left. His arm is bent at the elbow, creating the impression, intentionally or accidentally, that he is "showing" the scabbard to the woman, who turns as she flees, making gestures of entreaty.

13.   Bell-krater, once in the Roman market, by the Agrigento Painter (ARV^2 577,62; unpublished.)

The whereabouts of this vase is unknown to me. The ARV^2 caption reads: "A, youth with sword pursuing a woman".

14.   Fragment from the neck of a volute krater in Reggio by the Niobid Painter, late work (ARV^2 600,16; unpublished).

The only Reggio fragment from the neck of a volute krater by the Niobid Painter approximating the ARV^2 description bears the following representation. To the left (of the spectator) a woman; to her right, a youth moves to the right, that is, turning his back on her, a sword in his right hand. He wears only a cloak. What seems to be a fragment from the same neck, but not necessarily from the same side, shows a leg and part of a seated figure. Since the person attacked is missing, it is no more than an assumption that the youth is attacking a woman (see ARV^2 op.cit.), and that the scene belongs to the series under discussion. Assuming that the fragment with the seated figure belongs to the other side, the iconographical arrangement would probably resemble that on nos. 8, 29 and 30, which include a female spectator behind the attacking youth.

As I looked for this fragment in the storerooms of the Reggio Museum, I found another fragment apparently by the Niobid Painter, which does not appear to be included in ARV^2 or *Paralipomena* and which may be connected with the subject. A youth wearing a chiton moves to the right, scabbard hanging at his side; his arms and hands are missing, but the sword, of which a large part is preserved, was probably held in his right hand. Near the sword, part of a stick or staff is visible. Associated with the sword, as though clasped at the missing handle and hanging around the top of the blade, are peculiar lumps best described as looking like hunks of meat. I cannot imagine what they might be. But if they could indeed be pieces of meat, their representation here, clasped in the same hand as the sword, would fit admirably the Theseus-Medea story. According to Plut. *Thes.* xii, 2–3, Aigeus recognised his son's sword when Theseus took it from its scabbard to cut meat.

15. Hydria at Taranto by the Niobid Painter (ARV^2 606,74; unpublished).

The staff at the Taranto Museum, which I visited, were unable to locate this vase. The ARV^2 caption reads: "Youth with sword and spears pursuing a woman". For the commentary on the type of the youth with sword and spears see no. 16 below.

16. Hydria G 427 by the Geneva Painter[144] (ARV^2 615,2; Pottier pl. 142, CVA d pl. 52, 1–3;5).

This scene does not quite belong to the series. It shows a young man wearing chiton, cloak and a petasos thrown at the back of his neck, holding a drawn sword in his right hand and spears in his left, going after a woman who is starting to move away from him, making a startled gesture. Around the pair various other girls are also fleeing and making startled gestures. It seems to be the result of an iconographical conflation of two patterns: 1, that of a youth attacking a woman with a sword, that is, attempted murder; and 2, a youth with spears (and petasos and cloak) pursuing a woman, frequently in the presence of her companion, that is, erotic purusit. The youth in the second pattern is probably also Theseus,[145] but the identity of the woman is not established.

17. Stemless cup London E 128 by the Carlsruhe Painter (ARV^2 737,137; Ghali-Kahil, *Enlèv*. pl. liv).

On side A, a youth, sword in hand, is attacking a woman. On side B an identical woman is fleeing *away* from a king who is not pursuing. On both sides the woman turns as she flees, making identical gestures of supplication; arms and hands open, palms upwards. Given that side B has no other obvious interpretation, it is tempting to suggest that the sides are connected, A showing Medea being attacked by Theseus, and B showing Medea fleeing from Aigeus. This hypothesis might gain support if it is considered that the same iconographical scheme is repeated at least three more times by the vase-painter, on the stemless cups listed below as nos. 18, 19 and 20. On the tondos of all four cups a king is shown in the company of a Nike. If the above interpretation is correct, this could be Aigeus with a Nike, a scene which need not be mythological.

18. Stemless cup by the Carlsruhe Painter, once Deepdene, Hope T 177 (ARV^2 737,135; Tischbein i pl. 2

Identical iconographical scheme as no. 17. On A, the youth wears chiton, cloak and sandals, and a petas thrown at the back of his neck. The woman flees, making gestures of supplication identical with those abc On B, a similar woman flees from a king who is not pursuing her.

19. Stemless cup at Warsaw (ex Binental) by the Carlsruhe Painter (ARV^2 737,136; CVA Binental pl. 2.6 [= Pologne pl. 109]).

The iconographical scheme is identical with nos. 17, 18 and 20. The only difference is that the attacking youth wears a helmet.

20. Stemless cup Naples 2643 by the Carlsruhe Painter (ARV^2 737,134; unpublished).

The iconographical scheme is as nos. 17, 18 and 19. On A, a youth, wearing cloak, chiton and sandals (traces of a petasos can also be seen) pursues a woman, sword in his right hand; his left hand is extended under the cloak. The woman turns and makes gestures of supplication. Her stance and gestures are repeated in those of the woman on B, who flees from a king (ARV^2 misleadingly reads "woman running to king").

21. Stemless cup Arezzo 1428, 1430 and 1434 frr. by the Carlsruhe Painter (ARV^2 738,143; unpublished

The scheme of the decoration of this cup is different: the youth with a sword pursuing a woman is shown on the tondo.

22. Stemless cup on the Italian market by the Carlsruhe Painter (ARV^2 737,138; unpublished).

The whereabouts of this cup are unknown. According to ARV^2 the tondo shows a king and a Nike and A a youth with a sword pursuing a woman; the subject of B was not known to Beazley. It is quite likely that this cup had the same iconographical scheme as nos. 17, 18, 19 and 20.

23. Cup-skyphos Leningrad 1541 (St. 1620) near the Carlsruhe Painter (Peredolskaya pl. cix).

In the tondo a youth with a sword is shown about to attack a woman. He wears chiton and cloak and has a petasos thrown at the back of his neck; he is holding the sword in his right hand, while his left arm, which appears to be extended, disappears behind the woman's back. The woman has started to flee from the youth, but turns and makes a gesture of supplication with her left arm and hand.

24. Oinochoe once on the Basle Market (Munzen und Medaillen) by the Painter of the Brussels oinochoai (ARV^2 775,6; unpublished).

I could not trace the whereabouts or find a photograph of this vase. The ARV^2 caption reads: "Youth with sword pursuing a woman (Theseus and Aithra?)".

25. Skyphos Gotha 55 by one of the followers of Douris (ARV^2 804,69; *CVA* pl. 50,3–4).

The youth is naked but for a cloak thrown over his extended left arm and hand, he holds the sword in his right hand, scabbard hanging at his side. The woman, on side B, flees to an altar. She turns with her arm extended back toward the youth on A, hand open, palm upwards, in a gesture of supplication.

26. Skyphos in Mississipi by the Lewis Painter (ARV^2 974,26; *CVA* Robinson ii pl. 41.1a).

The youth holds the sword in his right hand; his left arm and hand are hidden under the cloak. The woman does not flee from the youth as on other vases but faces him, her right arm extended towards him, hand open, palm upwards, in supplication. Most important, in her left hand she holds a jug, confirming that she is Medea. Medea holds the phiale and jug in the scenes related to the poison attempt, and in the one vase picture showing the recognition is shown with the jug while the phiale has already been given to Theseus. But in this scene Medea has just dropped the jug in astonishment and terror. It may be asked why, if the jug characterises the woman as Medea, it is shown only in this scene. There is a very good reason. I argued briefly in n. 2 that the iconographical scheme usually adopted in this series of scenes for the representation of Theseus attacking a woman with a sword was a highly codified sign — at the formal level, system of signs. This opinion was based on characteristics of the scene already apparent or which will emerge in the course of this chapter as symptoms of high codification or of factors conducive to it: the chronologically highly concentrated popularity; the simplicity of the iconographical scheme, which shows that it could easily be decoded without explanatory signs; and the fact that an extract could replace and signify the whole scene, which presupposes high codification if intelligibility is to be achieved. One concomitant of high codification is that there is no need to spell out the identity of the protagonists through the addition of *ad hoc* signs. This is clearly valid when the codified sign itself is used, that is, the canonical iconographical scheme found in most scenes (which will be discussed further later in this chapter) even when it is elaborated by additional elements (for instance, the altar). But if the sign is altered and the scheme *modified*, as here, where Medea is not fleeing but facing Theseus, it becomes necessary to eliminate ambiguity by adding a sign (the jug) to make clear that the woman is Medea, and that the scene shows Theseus attacking Medea. It is likely that the jug was not included in the scheme but was used only as a *characterising* sign, because the attack took place after Medea had dropped the jug. In the version reflected in the Apulian bell-krater Schloss Fasanerie 179, Medea dropped the jug at the moment Aigeus recognised Theseus.

A jug held by a woman attacked by a youth cannot satisfactorily be explained in any other context. Amymone is involved in an *erotic* pursuit by Poseidon, who has a very distinct iconography. One cannot even think of contamination from Amymone scenes, since Amymone holds a hydria and not a jug. The same is true for all figures of girls involved with drawing water from a fountain (for instance, Polyxena).

The case for recognising Medea in the woman with the jug on the skyphos by the Lewis Painter is thus very strong.

27. Skyphos Bologna 490 by the Painter of Louvre CA 1849 (ARV^2 979,10; unpublished. I have consulted a photograph taken by Mrs L. Berge).

The movement is from right to left; the youth is shown in three-quarter back view, naked, sword in his right hand, scabbard hanging at his side, left arm extended towards the woman, index finger pointing at her. She turns as she flees, making a gesture of entreaty.

This scene is usually interpreted as Orestes killing Klytaimestra, because side A, where a youth attacks a man, is interpreted as Orestes killing Aegisthus. However, this interpretation is by no means certain. Even if it were correct, it would not necessarily follow that side B depicts a related subject: the woman in this scene is not characterised as Klytaimestra, by holding an axe for example, and there is no reason why the scene should not belong to our series. It cannot *a priori* be denied that the iconographical pattern under discussion, an "averted stepmatricide", may have been used to express the actual matricide of Klytaimestra. But the use of a well-established and popular iconographical pattern to depict a related topic, without any characterisation to differentiate the scene showing the related subject from the mainstream of representations of the established iconographical pattern would be very surprising.

28. Neck amphora in Naples, Museo di Capodimonte, by an undetermined artist in the group of Polygnotus (ARV^2 1058,117; unpublished).

The ARV^2 description of side B of the neck contains an error: the pursuing youth holds a *spear,* not a sword, in his right hand. Otherwise, the iconographical scheme is identical with that of our series. The youth wears petasos and cloak, and his left arm is extended under the cloak which covers it. It is probable that the single spear replaced the sword through a contamination from the theme of the erotic pursuit by a youth holding spears.

29. Pelike Louvre C 10811 by the Painter of the Louvre Centauromachy (ARV^2 1093,83; unpublished).

The youth, whose head, neck, and part of whose shoulders are missing, wears a cloak and sandals, and has a petasos thrown at the back of his neck. He moves to the right, sword in his right hand, scabbard in his left. He holds the scabbard end outwards, like Menelaos on the now lost neck amphora by the Oionokles Painter which was previously in the Hamilton Collection in Naples (ARV^2 647,15; Ghali-Kahil, *Enlèv.* pl. 51 To the right of the youth, the woman he is attacking flees and turns to look at him. On the left of the youth another woman is fleeing, this time to the left; she also turns to look towards him. This fleeing companion is a stock figure in pursuit and abduction scenes. Here she performs a compositional function, making the scene symmetrical. In fact, as she is present, the youth becomes the central figure, flanked by women moving away from him, and the two women form a frame for the aggressor.

30. Column krater on the Paris market by the Naples Painter (ARV^2 1097,19; Tillyard pl. 21,133).

The main group on side A of the youth (with cloak, sword in right hand, petasos thrown at the back of his neck) advancing against a woman who turns as she flees, making a gesture of supplication with her left hand, is flanked by two spectators: a fleeing girl to the left, a bearded king with a sceptre at the right. This may be interpreted in the same way as no. 8; Theseus and Medea, with Aigeus, and the stock figure of the girl, here fleeing, to balance the composition on the left.

31. Column krater Faenza I by the Duomo Painter (ARV^2 1118,12; unpublished).

The woman on side A flees to the right and turns, making a gesture of supplication. The youth holds the sword in his right hand, while with his left he clutches the scabbard. His left arm is bent at the elbow, so that the impression is given that he is "showing" the scabbard to the fleeing woman. (Compare no. 12 above

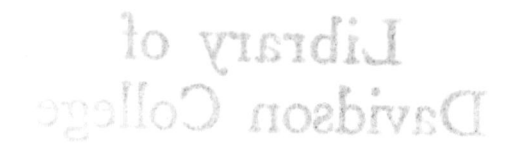

32. Pelike Munich 2354 (J 243) recalling the Hasselmann Painter (ARV^2 1139,2; *CVA* pl. 71.1; here **pl. 4**).

The youth, wearing chiton, cloak and sandals, with petasos thrown at the back of his neck, is rushing, sword in his right hand, toward a woman who turns back as she flees. (The scene is on side A.)

33. Cup Bologna 423, Submeidian group (the tondo) (ARV^2 1398,8; *CVA* pl. 133.3).

The youth wears sandals and has a petasos thrown at the back of his neck; he is naked, but has a wrap over his upper left arm. He holds the sword in his right hand, while with his left he grabs the woman by the hair, indicating violence. The woman opens both arms and hands in supplication. She is moving to the right, her movement arrested by the grabbing of her hair, and turning towards her aggressor. She stands before an altar, on which she had taken, or was about to take, refuge.

Another scene, on side A of the Nolan amphora London E 333 by the Sabouroff Painter (ARV^2 842,116; *CVA* pl. 64,2a; Ghali-Kahil, *Enlèv.* 85, pl. lii), differs from the rest of the series in one particular: the youth wears a corslet. He is beardless, with long hair, has a sword in his right hand, scabbard in his left, his left arm is extended and has a wrap thrown over it. He advances towards the fleeing woman. Ghali-Kahil[146] classified the scene as "type dérivé" from the theme "Menelaos pursuing Helen". Of course the youth is not Menelaos, since Menelaos is always shown bearded and mature. Variations of the same basic iconographical scheme are used for the three subjects: Menelaos attacking Helen; Odysseus attacking Circe; and Theseus attacking a woman I have identified as Medea. All are clearly differentiated. Theseus is a beardless youth, the other two attackers are bearded, mature men. In the scenes involving Odysseus and Circe which use the scheme[147] there is always at least one further element to make clear the identity of the participants: Circe holds or drops the skyphos in which she mixed her magic potion; often the stick with which she stirred the potion is also shown. Moreover, in some scenes Odysseus and Circe are flanked by Odysseus' companions, already transformed into pigs. With regard to Menelaos and Helen, the more generic scheme of a man pursuing a woman with drawn sword[148] appears early in the series (Ghali-Kahil's type i.b.a); but the specific scheme closely parallelled in the series of Theseus and Medea and Odysseus and Circe appears very infrequently.[149] When it does so, it is differentiated negatively: the pursuer is bearded and mature, which excludes Theseus, and the woman is not holding or dropping a skyphos, which excludes Circe.[150] Menelaos is sometimes, but not always, dressed as a warrior, with helmet, corslet and helmet, or corslet, helmet and greaves. Given that it is the lack of beard and the youth of the pursuer which identify him as Theseus, the scene on London E 333 must depict Theseus attacking Medea. The addition of the corslet is surely due to an iconographical contamination from the related theme "Menelaos attacking Helen". It is not a significant contamination, for the corslet was not an element *characterising* Menelaos in that theme, and so its introduction in a scene involving Theseus would not have produced ambiguity. I shall, however, exclude this scene from the main series.[151]

It is important to note that the three subjects — Theseus and Medea, Odysseus and Circe, and Menelaos and Helen — are related thematically as well as iconographically. If my identification of Medea as the woman attacked by Theseus be accepted, the similarity at the level of the signifier corresponds to a similarity at the level of the signified: the three subjects are concerned with the averted murder of a perfidious woman by a man whom she had wronged. At the iconographical level, Theseus and Medea and Odysseus and Circe are more closely related to each other than either is to Menelaos and Helen. While "Helen and Menelaos" uses sporadically the common iconographical scheme, both the others are consistently depicted by means of that scheme. This closer similarity at the level of the signifier corresponds to a closer similarity at the level of the signified: the antagonist of both Theseus and Odysseus was a sorceress, a polarisation of the concept "perfidious woman", indicating that the iconographical scheme here discussed came to acquire an even more specialised meaning, used consistently for the theme "averted murder of a sorceress by a man whom she had wronged". (Though it could still be used for the wider "averted murder of a perfidious woman by a man whom she had wronged".)

Let us now consider whether the detailed examination of scenes showing Theseus attacking a woman has confirmed or invalidated the hypothesis that they represent Theseus attacking Medea. Since it is clear that those scenes representing the attack in the most elementary terms of the iconographical pattern, offer no evidence other than that already discussed, we should dwell on additional iconographical element

I shall start with a doubtful additional element, since it is found in the scene with which this whole discussion started, on the tondo of the Makron cup. The fact that the spears are resting against the background could suggest that the attack began while the hero had been resting, having put down his spears. But the spears may have been added only because they were part of the Theseus iconography, and shown resting because if he were holding them Theseus would have appeared overburdened. The same problem is posed by the tondo of the cup by the Penthesilea Painter, where the club and pilos rest in a corner. They may have been put there with the intention of underlining the identity of the youth as Theseus, but they may also have been intended to suggest an attack during a restful occasion, as opposed to an immediate attack. In the latter case, the spears and the club and the pilos may offer a small corroboration in favour of the "Theseus attacking Medea" hypothesis: the attempted poisoning which triggered off the attack took place while Theseus was the guest of Aigeus and Medea.

Another element of doubtful significance is the altar. The fact that some scenes include an altar at which the attacked woman tries to take refuge does not necessarily entail that a point of refuge was mentioned in the story they reflect. It may have been added through a purely iconographical association of ideas: a woman is murderously attacked and flees while making gestures of supplication; people in danger of their lives take refuge at altars, and so do suppliants; so an altar would make iconographical sense and may have been added for no other reason. However, if the scenes represent a specific story, as they must do, it would be unlikely that an altar would have been added, unless this thematic motif was included in the story. Its inclusion in the scenes may suggest its inclusion in the story.

On the Adolphseck krater, which must reflect a tragedy, the recognition takes place around an altar at which Theseus makes a libation. *A priori*, this altar may have been shown in the scene because it was included in the story, or because it was part of the stage décor. The altar involved in the action in some Greek plays is not the altar of Dionysus in the orchestra, but a special stage altar. Some scholars believe that it was a portable property altar,[152] and others that it was a permanent structure, used when needed by the plot, and otherwise ignored.[153] It is reasonable to believe that if an altar is shown on a vase depicting a scene from a tragedy, then the altar was somehow included in the action. Not all vase-paintings with scenes from tragedy include an altar, so the altar shown on the Adolphseck krater with the recognition scene is likely to have been included in the story, confirmed by the fact that Theseus is shown pouring a libation on this altar. The inclusion of the altar might thus provide a little confirmation for the interpretation that the scenes show Theseus' attack on Medea after the recognition: the altar's presence can find a satisfactory explanation in the framework of this interpretation, since it appears in the earlier sequences, and was probably included in the action. But the frequency with which altars appear in Greek plays and stories weakens the strength of this confirmation.

Another element which may be considered as supporting the Theseus-**Medea** hypothesis is the figure of the bearded king. Female spectators in general, and fleeing or startled maidens in scenes of attack, abduction or pursuit in particular, are stock iconographical motifs which may be interpreted in various ways — as characters added to the story (iconographically or otherwise) at will.[154] But that is not true of the king, who appears as an interested spectator on nos. 8 and 30, and who must be considered as having a specific significance. And there is a king who is relevant, though not indispensable, to the attack of Theseus against Medea: Aigeus, the third main figure in events preceding the attack. In a few cups by the Carlsruhe Painter, on the reverse of the scene showing a youth attacking a woman, is represented a king from whom a woman flees. If the two sides are related, and the repetition of the scheme may suggest that they are, Theseus and Medea on the obverse, with Medea fleeing from Aigeus on the reverse, is the only interpretation which fits the picture. It would then be legitimate to claim that the king from whom the woman flees in these cups is the king who appears as an interested spectator on nos. 8 and 30. Aigeus would suit both roles. But even independently of the Carlsruhe Painter's cups, I can think of no king whose presence in the scenes of the attack would make sense as an interested spectator, and not as a prospective victim, as Aegisthus would be. Nor can I think of any other explanation for the scene showing a woman making gestures of supplication as she runs from a king who does not pursue her.

The one iconographical element which argues very strongly in favour of the interpretation is the jug held by the woman in the skyphos by the Lewis Painter. This jug can only have the function of characterising the woman as Medea in the course of events after Theseus' arrival in Athens and connected with the poison attempt.

It should be noted in a discussion of iconographical motifs that two scenes, nos. 8 and 33, include the motif of grabbing by the hair, suggesting a murderous attack. This confirms that the attack on the woman was treated iconographically as being very serious, involving life and death, although not all victims grabbed by the hair are murdered: Kassandra, who was to be sacrilegously raped, was also grabbed by the hair by Ajax the Locrian.

On the Oxford hydria fragment (no. 7) the youth is either sheathing or unsheathing his sword. If he is unsheathing it, no additional information can be gained. But the fact that the attacking youth seems to be moving away from the fleeing woman probably indicates that the attack is over, unless the figures now missing altered the scene's complexion, which appears unlikely. In that case the scene would show an attack which did not culminate in murder, which would suit the Medea theme.

If the youth in no. 27 is meant to be pointing his finger at the fleeing woman, since the scene is one of attack, he must be doing so in accusation. This fits the Theseus-Medea story well; Theseus would be accusing Medea: "So it is you who persuaded my father to try and kill me". It would, of course, also suit any other story in which the attack of the youth is the result of a previous action of the woman against the youth. But the Theseus-Medea interpretation may provide an iconographical parallel: the accusatory pointing by Theseus at the probable Medea on the Bactrian bowl.

There is thus quite a strong case for interpreting the scenes under discussion as Theseus attacking Medea after the attempted poisoning.[155]

I have listed thirty-three scenes showing Theseus attacking Medea (thirty-four if London E 333 is included). The Makron cup and the Myson oinochoe are the earliest. Makron's work belongs basically to the generation *ca* 500 to 480. The Leningrad cup with Theseus is probably a late work of the artist, to be placed probably a little after 480, and Myson's scene should be dated between *ca* 480 and 475. Of the remaining thirty-one scenes, twenty-six (twenty seven with London E 333) were painted in the 460s and between the 460s and the 440s. Only five are later, of which four were painted by artists working between *ca* 450 and 425, and only one is much later, Submeidian. It is clear then that the scenes with Theseus attacking Medea are very heavily concentrated in the twenty years or so between the 460s and the 440s.

Most of these representations follow the same iconographical pattern: a youth advancing upon a woman, sword in his right hand, the woman fleeing to the right (of the spectator), turning towards the youth and making gestures of supplication. Minor variations occur: the youth may be wearing a chiton and cloak, or a cloak alone, or he can have just a wrap thrown over part of his body. He can wear the petasos, normally thrown at the back of his neck, or less frequently, the pilos. The scabbard may hang at his side, or he may be holding it in his left hand. I shall call this iconographical scheme "the pattern" or "the scheme", and consider how many scenes follow this "pattern", how many use a modified or extended version, and how many are totally unrelated.

Scenes taken into account: twenty-nine. A thirtieth, no. 21, I have not been able to see. Scenes the whereabouts of which are unknown to me: three.

Of the two earliest representations, the Makron cup shows no relation to, or awareness of, the pattern. The Myson oinochoe, also from the 470s, is related to the later pattern. The balance of the composition is different on this oinochoe. In the overwhelming majority of the scenes the youth and the woman are shown alone. In two cases they are flanked by two spectators, again making them equipollent central elements. In one later example by the Painter of the Louvre Centauromachy, the centre of the compositi is the youth, flanked on one side by the woman he is attacking, on the other by another woman fleeing in the opposite direction, so the scene remains symmetrical. Myson's scene is unbalanced; from the poin of view of thematic composition, the youth to the left corresponds to the two fleeing women to the right The fleeing companion at the extreme right is a stock figure in scenes of erotic pursuit and abduction to which also belong the two or more maidens fleeing in the same direction away from the pursuing youth. It appears that the scene on the Boston oinochoe was influenced by and based on the iconography of erotic pursuit. It should be noted that the youth wears neither petasos nor pilos, and it therefore cannot be excluded, although it is not very likely, that the scene may not represent Theseus at all.[156]

Of the other twenty-seven scenes, thirteen (fourteen if London E 333 is included), show the "pattern" "scheme" in its simple and unadulterated form. On no. 6 the "scheme" is split between the vase's two sides. Two show the pattern with the addition of an altar: on no. 25 the scheme is again split between the two sides. One shows the "pattern" with additional altar and with the youth grabbing the woman by the hair. Two show the simple pattern modified in that the movement is from right to left. One (perhaps two, with fragment no. 14 uncertain) shows the pattern with the addition of a spectator on each side. One adds a fleeing companion; one more modifies the pattern to movement from right to left, with the grabbing by the hair motif and two spectators. Two are contaminated from the theme "youth with spears pursuing a woman", and a third is contaminated from the same theme only in so far as the youth's weapon is a single spear instead of a sword; in every other respect that scene (no. 28) follows the "scheme One shows a modified "pattern": the youth as normal but the woman (who is holding a jug) does not flee but faces the aggressor, making a gesture of supplication. Finally, one fragmentary scene, no. 7, betrays no relation to the "pattern"; but then it represents a different moment in the action, and was painted by a Mannerist.[157]

Of the twenty-nine scenes considered, thirteen show the simple "pattern", nine show the "pattern" with minor additions or very minor changes, and in one the "pattern" is minimally contaminated from another scene (no. 28, in the weapon). Two are contaminated from that same theme; two, one of which lies at the beginning of the series, are unrelated to the "scheme"; one has modified the scheme; and one (no. 2) is "related" to the "scheme".

The iconography of this scene is clearly remarkably consistent with the "scheme" showing a tenacious persistence in the overwhelming majority of cases. As is apparent in the table,[157] the use of the "scheme" transcends workshop divisions and is found on the vases of artists working in different workshops. Moreover, once established, its use persists to the latest vase decorated with the subject, the Submeidian cup Bologna 423. This remarkable frequency, persistent appearance in the works of otherwise unrelated artists, and continuity of use through about three-quarters of a century into a period in which the representation of the subject had become rare, suggests that a prototype may have been available for imitation and inspiration outside the narrow limits of one workshop. This can mean only a prototype in "major" art, a painting or a relief, perhaps a free-standing sculptural group which would have allowed the high codification of the scene and the means for the preservation of the codified sign at a time when it was rarely depicted in vase-painting. The existence of a prototype in major art would also make it easier to understand the process by which this iconographical scheme came to acquire, within the code of Greek iconography, the specialised meaning "averted murder of a sorceress by a man who had been wronged by her". To the basic "pattern" established through that prototype minor iconographic elements were sometimes added: an altar, the motif of grabbing the woman by the hair, one or two spectators. Their addition does not alter the meaning of the scheme or produce ambiguity. The presence of the altar and the motif of grabbing by the hair increase the intensity of the attack portrayed. The change in direction of the movement found in a few scenes is a "stylistic variant"[158] that is a variant motivated by a purely aesthetic, not semiological, choice. The addition of the stock figures of the two spectators, making the scheme more elaborate, produces another such stylistic variant. It is interesting to note that the addition of the two spectators and the change in direction of the movement can be combined, as in no. 8. If there was a prototype in major art, it was probably painted or sculpted after Makron's cup; certainly that cup bears no relation to the "scheme". The connection between the "scheme" and Myson's scene is more problematic: Myson's is a rudimentary version in which the iconography of the erotic pursuit/abduction has been adapted to show an attack, but his scene is connected as the type of composition that will later crystallise into the "scheme". Was that because the iconographic prototype had already been painted or sculpted? If so, the divergences from the "scheme" and similarities with the erotic pursuit/abduction would be due to Myson's choice of mixing the borrowed elements of the prototype with iconographic elements from his traditional vase-painter's repertory. The occasion of the commission of the prototype could have been the transfer of Theseus' bones from Skyros to Athens.[159] If that is the case, the fact that no representation of the subject survives between Myson and the 460s, despite the establishment of the prototype, cannot satisfactorily be explained through the accident of preservation when we consider the number of specimens from the 460s to the 440s. But it could be that the iconographic prototype did not have an immediate and direct impact on vase-painting, and that the popularity of the subject from the 460s was due to a different, non-iconographic factor — and in fact I shall be claiming below that in any case it was a non iconographical factor, a play, that caused that remarkable boom of the subject between the 460s and the 440s. On this hypothesis, it would be only when the subject had become popular through the play that the vase-painters would have turned to that prototype of the 470s to draw formal inspiration for the pictorial representation of the subject. I find this alternative implausible. It is much more likely that the prototype had not been created when Myson painted his oinochoe. The similarities between his scene and that which became canonical are probably the result of the facts that on the one hand Myson's scene is an adaptation of the "erotic pursuit" scheme, and on the other that the generic pattern usually chosen by Greek iconography for depicting a man attacking a woman with a sword, on which this specific iconographic scheme is based, is iconographically related to that of erotic pursuit. It is thus reasonable to conclude that both the prototype in major art[160] and the great boom in the representation of the subject on vases were triggered in the early 460s by the same event.

That the scene of a youth attacking a woman with a sword was highly codified is also shown by the fact that "extracts" from it, which may be taken as meaning to convey the idea of the whole scene, signifying the whole through one of its parts in a metonymic relationship (see n. 2), were painted. The following representations I interpret as such "excerpts".

1.   Nolan amphora Leyden PC 86 (xviii h 39) by the Providence Painter (ARV^2 637,38; *OudhedMedel* 62[1961] pl. 13a). The stance of the youth is very similar to that of the youth on no. 3 above, also by the Providence Painter, but in the extract he wears a chiton as well as having a wrap over his extended left arm.

2.   Lekythos Oxford 1916.15 by the Carlsruhe Painter (ARV^2 733,71; *CVA* i, pl. 38.1); (see also lekythos Athens E 1842 [ARV^2 733,72]). A Doric column shown at the left indicates a house. In front of it a youth, naked but for cloak and sandals, petasos thrown at the back of his neck, moves to the right, sword in hand. His left arm is extended and covered by the cloak; part of it is missing.

3.   Neck-amphora in the Berlin market in the manner of Hermonax (ARV^2 493,3). A youth attacking with a sword is shown on side B; Beazley (ARV^2 op.cit.) compares this representation with the scene on no. 6 above, the Nolan amphora by Hermonax, where the "scheme" is divided between the two sides.

4.   Unattributed lekythos New York 41.162.206, middle of the fifth century (*CVA* Gallatin pl. 59.4). The youth has no petasos; he wears a chiton, has a cloak over his extended left arm, and a sword in his right hand.

5.   Lekythos New York 41.162.15 by the Oionokles Painter (*ARV*^{2} 648,39; *CVA* Gallatin pl. 16.1).

6.   Lekythos in Gela by the Oionokles Painter (*ARV*^{2} 648,38). It should be noted that the Oionokles Painter is a follower of the Providence Painter.

7.   Cup Tarquinia RC 2072 by the Sabouroff Painter (*ARV*^{2} 837,2; *CVA* pl. 19). On the tondo a youth, naked but for a cloak, petasos thrown at the back of his neck, scabbard hanging at his left side, advances to the right, drawn sword in his right hand, left arm extended under the cloak. The youth is similar to the one on no. 11 of the main series, also by the Sabouroff Painter. But here he is moving from left to right, as is canonical in the series, and has the petasos at the back of his neck, again much more usual than the pilos of the Louvre tondo.

8.   Lekythos Munich 2500 by the Cairo Group (related to the Carlsruhe Painter), (*ARV*^{2} 740; *EAA* ii, 256, fig. 384). A youth, naked but for cloak and sandals, petasos slung at the back of his neck, advances to the right, drawn sword in his right hand, left arm extended under the cloak which covers it.

9.   Two recently published lekythoi attributed by Buschor to the Carlsruhe Painter; the suggestion by A.B. Follmann that they belong together may perhaps confirm my hypothesis that the attacking youth, sword in hand, is an excerpt from, and may stand for, the scene in question. The lekythoi are published in *Antiken aus Rheinischem Privatbesitz* (Cologne 1973) nos. 63.1 and 63.2 (p. 47, pl. 28). The comments by Follmann, implies that they were found in the same Attic grave. They are identical in shape, size, scheme of decoration and ornament. These circumstances led Follmann to believe that they form a set, and that the youth shown on one lekythos is pursuing the woman depicted on the other. On lekythos 1, the youth advances to the right; he wears a cloak, has the petasos thrown at the back of his neck and the sword in his right hand, his extended left arm is covered by the cloak. On lekythos 2, the woman turns as she flees, and makes gestures of supplication.

The splitting of the scene over two vases is a significant and decisive advancement from splitting it over the two sides of one vase. For this to have happened the individual figures must have acquired some measure of autonomy. The isolated figure of the fleeing supplicant woman is a "syllabogram" rather than an ideogram, fitting into many subjects involving attack or pursuit. The youth, with petasos and cloak, moving to the right, sword in hand, occurs only on his own outside the scenes under discussion: this figure does not form a consistent element of any other scene. With the two new lekythoi he can now be placed in three contexts: i, in the scene discussed; ii, alone; iii, in between, on his own but forming part of the scene, split over two vases. Type iii, which encompasses parts of both i and ii, suggests that ii should also be seen as "part" of i, that is, as conveying i whether or not some scenes of type ii may originally also have been parts of a complete set. It suggests that the lone youth attacking with a sword was indeed an "extract" from the scenes and was understood as such. There appears to be confirmation in the fact that all the "extracts" attributed to individual painters — only one remains unattributed — were made either by artists who painted, often more than once, the complete scene of a youth attacking a woman with a sword: the Carlsruhe Painter, the Providence Painter, the Sabouroff Painter, Hermonax (the extract in his manner, perhaps by him), and, as I shall argue below, the Penthesilea Painter; or, in the case of the Oionokles Painter, who painted two "excerpts", by an artist associated with a vase-painter who had painted the complete scene. Of the first group, the Carlsruhe Painter depicted the full subject six times, with a seventh specimen "near" him, plus once split over the two lekythoi, and twice he painted the attacking youth on his own. The artists who painted Theseus attacking a woman with a sword could hardly have failed to conceive of a youth they showed dressed like Theseus, in the stance of Theseus, and performing the same action as Theseus in the full scene, as Theseus, indeed as Theseus in the course of his attack against the woman, in fact, as an "excerpt" from the iconographical theme "Theseus attacking a woman with a sword".[161]

I should also like to recognise an "excerpt" of the theme of Theseus attacking Medea after the recognition in two of the figures on the Ferrara cup T 18C VP (ARV^2 882,35; Alfieri, *RIA* 8 [1959] 59–110; Alfieri/Arias, *Spina* pl. 28). The two figures are an old king with a sceptre (in this context he must be Aigeus), who moves towards Theseus and holds his himation with his right hand; and Theseus himself, petasos thrown at the back of his neck. He moves to the right, sword upright in his right hand, but has momentarily arrested his movement to turn back toward the old king as he leans partly on the spear he holds in front of him. These figures, depicted between the episode of the Marathonian bull and that of the Minotaur, are usually considered as belonging to the episode of the bull. It is usually thought that this episode is narrated in three successive scenes: Theseus starting for Marathon in the presence of Aigeus; Theseus leading the defeated bull to Athens; and two legendary Athenian kings. But there are several objections to this interpretation. First, no other episode in the cycle is analysed in more than one scene, although several could have been split or extended more profitably and with more reason than the bull deed. Examples are Sinis and his daughter, who are combined in one scene, and the adventure of the Minotaur, which could have been extended to include Ariadne and her ball of thread. In any event, setting out for the encounter with the bull was not an important part of the story. Second, if the three scenes did belong together, and did show an analysed form of the bull adventure, their chronological order would be from left to right, the opposite order from that followed for the whole of the cycle. If we consider the relative positions of the bull adventure and the Minotaur struggle, the latter and the cycle of deeds on the road from Troezen to Athens, and this last and the episode of the bull again, it is clear that for the whole of the cycle the chronological order is from right to left. Last, in this "setting out" scene which I interpret as an excerpt, the sword is given prominence with the spear in second place, while in the bull episode Theseus in this period is given only the club, and no other weapon; it would be rather peculiar if the "setting out" scene portrayed weapons not used in the adventure on which the hero was setting out and did not show the one weapon which was to be used in the struggle. It is in the recognition episode that the sword is prominent, as well as in the attack upon Medea.

The so-called three scenes from the bull adventure can more satisfactorily be explained in the following way. First, the figures of Aigeus and Theseus are an "excerpt" of the scene of the attack against Medea. It is strange but not inexplicable that the figure of Medea is missing. If the scene of the attack was indeed well known and popular, the excerpt would convey to the spectator the whole scene as well as hinting at the recognition; and in the context of the glorification of Theseus as an Athenian hero the figures of Theseus himself and of Aigeus were important, and not that of Medea, although I shall suggest below a politico-propaganda significance for the scene of the attack against her. Second, taken together as one scene, Theseus would be seen leading the defeated bull to Aigeus and a legendary Attic king, or to Aigeus and an Athenian "elder" representing the Athenian people.[162]

This interpretation would restore a chronological and iconographical balance to the representation of Theseus' adventures. I consider the beginning of the cycle to be at the left of the Minotaur, and the struggle with the Minotaur would be the last deed portrayed, as it was Theseus' last "deed" in the traditional sense. Beginning at the left of the Minotaur, just under and to the left of the left handle, the death of Sinis is shown as the first of Theseus' deeds, on the road from Troezen to Athens. Between the handles is developed this cycle of deeds on the road to Athens. It does not follow the order in which they appear in the literary tradition but shows: i. Sinis; ii. Procroustes; iii. Kerkyon; iv. Sow; v. Skiron; that of the literary tradition: i. Sinis; ii. Sow; iii. Skiron; iv. Kerkyon; v. Procroustes. This cycle of deeds on the road to Athens ends just beyond the right handle. Between the two handles on the other side are three separate episodes following Theseus' arrival in Athens: the Marathonian bull; the recognition of Theseus by Aigeus as his son and Theseus' attack on Medea; and the victory over the Minotaur, which sealed Theseus' career as a young hero.

If this recognition of the scenes as "excerpts from the scenes showing Theseus attacking Medea" is correct, confirmation is gained for the popularity of these representations and especially for the popularity of the iconographical scheme which I call "the pattern", since the representation of part of it was sufficient to convey the whole theme, through a metonymic relationship.[163]

48

6. Words, pictures and meanings

A stage in the enquiry has now been reached at which the following question must be asked: Did the iconographical theme of Theseus attacking Medea after the recognition have any specific "ideological" value, did it convey any meaning to the spectator beyond the immediate mythological motif? Did it convey any value and meaning of the type of that, for example, attached to the scenes showing Amazonomachies, Centauromachies or Trojan Wars, which are iconographical themes standing for the Persian Wars and the triumph of Greece and culture over the East and barbarism? The significant way to phrase the question is as follows: Is there any nexus of ideas beyond the immediate one of mythological narrative associated with the theme "Theseus attacking Medea", which is automatically conveyed to the mind of the contemporary spectator at the sight of this scene?

Two facts seem to indicate *a priori* that there was indeed an "ideological" dimension in the scenes, insofar as their presence can be considered the corollary of the existence of an ideological dimension

First, the popularity of a mythological scene of no special decorative value, and especially the very heavy concentration of the representations between the 460s and the 440s. This cannot be invalidated by the invocation of the iconographical prototype in major art suggested above; we would still have to ask the following two questions: why was this prototype painted or sculpted in the first place, in that period when art was to a great extent ideological; and what was it about the subject of this prototype that caused it so often to be imitated in vase-painting in that period?

Second, the fact that the figure of Theseus could be shown on its own while still conveying to the spectator the whole theme. For this to occur it is necessary that the scene should be well known and popular. But such popularity does not necessarily explain why such an excerpt should be considered worthy of depiction, especially within the representation of the whole Theseus cycle, as on the Penthesilea Painter's cup. The fact that it was may perhaps suggest that the theme had a meaning other than merely an iconographical or narrative-mythological value to convey, a value functioning beyond the narrative level and therefore "ideological", to conjure which the "iconogram" of the single figure was sufficient.

Whether any such "ideological" value can in fact be detected in the theme of Theseus attacking Medea must now be considered.

There is immediately the general ideological/political/propaganda significance of the whole of the Theseus legend. He was the Athenian hero *par excellence* and for this reason themes from his life were popular in Athenian iconography; Athens was glorified through the heroic deeds of Theseus, and Athenian iconography had a predilection for the representation of these deeds. Kimon in particular promoted the figure of Theseus for politico-propaganda reasons;[164] under his influence, in the years under consideration Theseus subjects became very popular not only on vases but also in major art.[165] The emergence or boost in popularity of any iconographical theme from the Theseus cycle thus fits very well in the context of the years following the Persian Wars. But not even the general political climate and the importance of Theseus in this period explain the emergence and popularity of this mythological and iconographical motif, which tells of no great heroic deed. So there must be some specific "ideological" value attached to *this particular motif*.[166]

To consider the story again: there are two protagonists, Theseus, *the* Athenian hero, who fought with the Athenians against the Persians at Marathon, and Medea, the Kolchis sorceress who before going to Athens had lived, in far from happy circumstances, at Iolkos and Corinth. Since Theseus is concerned with her departure, or rather exile, from Athens, it may be instructive to consider what happened to her after she left. And this is where a very peculiar story must be considered:

> (See also the *testimonia* quoted above in Chapter 4, pp. 22 ff., Dion. Per. 1020–8, Diod. iv.55,4–7, Eustath. Comm. on Diod. Per. 1017,20, and Apollod. i.ix.28.)

Hdt. vii. 62

> οἱ δὲ Μῆδοι...ἐκαλέοντο δὲ πάλαι πρὸς πάντων
> Ἄριοι, ἀπικομένης δὲ Μηδείης τῆς Κολχίδος ἐξ
> Ἀθηνέων ἐς τοὺς Ἀρίους τούτους μετέβαλον καὶ οὗτοι
> τὸ οὔνομα. αὐτοὶ περὶ σφέων ὧδε λέγουσι Μῆδοι.

Pausan. ii.iii,8

> ...ἐξ Ἀθηνῶν ἔφυγε, παραγενομένη δὲ ἐς τὴν
> λεγομένην τότε Ἀρίαν τοῖς ἀνθρώποις ἔδωκε τὸ
> ὄνομα καλεῖσθαι Μήδους ἀπ' αὐτῆς. τὸν δὲ παῖδα,
> ὃν ἐπήγετο φεύγουσα ἐς τοὺς Ἀρίους, γενέσθαι λέγουσιν
> ἐξ Αἰγέως, ὄνομα δὲ οἱ Μῆδον εἶναι.

Hygin. *Fab*. xxvii

> ...Medus ... ex suo nomine terram Mediam cognominavit.

(cf. also *Fab*. xxvi)

It is impossible, of course, to believe Herodotus' claim that it was the Medes themselves who believed this to be the origin of their name. The non-Hellenised form of the name of the Medes was not very close to the word Μήδεια.[167] There can be no doubt that the story and the false etymology were created in Greek circles. The attribution to the Medes appears to be an attempt at authentication.

When this story, which associates Medea with the Medes and Persians, the enemies of Greece, first made its appearance is not known, but there is a *terminus ante quem* in Herodotus. It is probably reasonable to assume that it appeared at a time when the Greeks were interested in the Medes and Persians, that is, during the Persian Wars or the years following them.

In the light of this story, the theme can now be seen in the following terms. Theseus the Athenian hero chased out of Attica at the point of his sword Medea, an Oriental woman closely connected with the Medes, and thus in general with the Persian enemy. This theme would have been seen as symbolising the Greek victory over Persia, and more specifically, the Athenian contribution to that victory. It would suit perfectly the mythological mentality of the years following the Persian Wars. In those years many myths which could be perceived as containing the concept of "victory of civilisation over barbarism", like Centauromachies (Greek heroes defeating undisciplined half-monsters) and Amazonomachies (Greek male heroes defeating Oriental women) were similarly reinterpreted: they came to be seen as symbolic expressions of the historical conflict between Greece and Persia perceived by the Greeks as precisely such a victory of civilisation over barbarism. In fact, the myth of Theseus and Medea could offer even more: it could also be seen as an actual mythological prefiguration of the historical conflict. This becomes clear when episodes from the Theseus cycle after the hero's arrival in Athens are considered side by side with the historical events of the first quarter of the fifth century.

1. **Medea** persuades Aigeus to send **Theseus** to do a deed intended as a **deadly trap** for the hero: to go to **Marathon** and capture a dangerous bull.	1. The **Persians** attack Greece, with **Athens** as one of their prime targets. Athens is in **deadly danger**. The confrontation takes place at **Marathon**.
2. **Against all odds, Theseus** emerges **victorious** from the conflict with the beast.	2. **Against all odds, the Athenians** emerge **victorious** from the battle (and Theseus was said to have appeared and assisted them during that battle).
3. **Medea** makes a **second** murderous attempt against **Theseus**: she tries to poison him.[168]	3. The **Persians** mount a **second** expedition against **Greece**.
4. But Aigeus recognises Theseus as his son, the **murder of the hero is averted**, and **Medea** is **chased out of Attica**. She **goes** to the **land of the Medes**.	4. The **Greeks** fight the Persians and emerge **victorious**. After Salamis, where the victory is due primarily to the Athenians, the Persian king **flees to Persia**, the Persian fleet and a large part of the army withdraws from Greece. The troops that remain are **again defeated** the next year, at Plataea, and the Persian **threat** against Greece **vanishes**. (A two-stage "victory" and "expulsion" theme here.)

It is clear that the correspondence between legend and historical events is very close, and indeed, too close and neat to be due to coincidence. It must be the result of a conscious manipulation of the legend aimed at transforming this myth into the mythological prefiguration at the conflict between Greece and Persia.

Before details of this reshaping and reinterpretation are considered, it should be noted that a manipulation of this kind can have taken place only in a literary product. Of course, the new version of the legend left its imprint on the popular mythological vision.[169]

Another point that must be made now is that in the table of correspondences between historical events and myth Theseus' attack on Medea and her expulsion from Attica correspond to the final expulsion of the Persians from Greece. While in history the final victory over the Persians was the result of a co-operative effort of several Greek states, in myth the equivalent action is centred on the figure of Theseus (who stands for Athens). This divergence, far from upsetting the suggested balance, is very easily explained in terms of Athenian, and more specifically Kimonian, propaganda in the years after the Persian Wars. This propaganda (subsequently, at least partly, embodied in the Athenian "image" of the city's own history) distorted the historical events to some extent by spotlighting parts of the picture and relegating others into comparative darkness. It exalted Marathon at the expense of the events of the "second expedition"; Marathon was presented as a victory of the Athenians alone, with virtually no mention of the Plataean contribution. This, the Athenian character of the victory, was one reason why Marathon became the *topos* of Athenian propaganda. The other relates to the political circle which promoted the Marathon "legend", the Kimonian party. Apart from the personal advantage derived by Kimon through the glorification of his father's victory, there was also party interest in minimising Salamis, the victory of Themistokles and the democratic party, in favour of Marathon, won by the aristocrats without entailing the sacrifice of leaving Athens open to devastation and destruction.[170]

Although mechanically the motif of Theseus attacking Medea and expelling her from Attica represents the final expulsion of the Persians, in which Athens played only a partial role, it also represents the more generic, propagandistic, and historically inaccurate theme of Athens expelling the Persians and saving Greece, a theme which operated through the exaltation of Marathon and perhaps to a lesser extent of Eurymedon, and the minimisation of the other victories.

To return to the legend of Theseus and to consider in some detail the manipulation of the legend, the state of the legend before the manipulation must first be ascertained. There is reason to believe that the story of the attempted murder of Theseus by Aigeus had been invented in the late sixth century *Theseid*. I shall now attempt to reconstruct the early form of this story.

First, the bull adventure. Not all sources present this episode as part of the murder attempt against Theseus. Some[171] show Theseus fighting the bull after the recognition, and not before, and on his own initiative rather than sent by Medea as part of the attempt to kill him. There can be little doubt that the early version is the one which treats the bull adventure as an independent, youthful deed of the hero, for the following reasons. Theseus is shown fighting the bull on a black-figure vase of the second quarter of the sixth century,[172] that is, earlier than the *Theseid*. Since there is reason to believe that the murder plot made its first appearance in the *Theseid*, the independent adventure version is earlier than that which makes the expedition against the Marathonian bull part of the plot. The most likely context for the creation of the latter variant is the manipulation which reinterpreted the theme of the murder plot against Theseus and made the conflict of Theseus and Medea signify the victory of Greece over Persia. In that context the defeat at Marathon of the bull, and thus also of the Oriental sorceress' plot, corresponds to the Persian defeat at Marathon. It was a crucial part of the reinterpretation that the defeat of the bull at Marathon should also be a defeat of the Oriental sorceress associated with and representing the Persian enemy; this was possible only if the expedition against the bull was not an independent deed but part of the plot devised by Medea for the destruction of Theseus. The manipulation provides the only context in which the transformation of an independent deed into a trap intended to be deadly makes perfect sense. The correlation between the bull adventure presented as part of the plot and the historical events is so perfect that it must be due to manipulation, even if the argument that it is earlier than the *Theseid* and thus earlier than the invention of the murder plot itself is discarded. Otherwise a very implausible coincidence would have to be postulated.

It seems then, that the bull adventure was presented as an independent youthful deed before the manipulation which reinterpreted the legend in an historical key, and that it was as such that it was incorporated in the *Theseid*.

It is impossible to know whether the bull adventure had been set at Marathon before the manipulation. If not, it could easily have been transferred there by the author of the manipulation to provide the first correspondence with historical events. If, as is more likely, the adventure was already placed at Marathon, the "manipulation" would have operated more naturally. A story already established in its general lines was not altered but its position in the legend and thus its function was changed and that part of the pattern of the story recast to correspond to the historical events it was to symbolise. It should be noted that the motif of the hero fighting a wild beast lent itself to this type of reinterpretation. Like the fight of the hero with a Centaur, it expresses the struggle between the civilised and the uncivilised. The victory of Theseus over the bull was well suited to symbolising the Greek victory, which was seen in this light.

Was Medea introduced into the story as Theseus' stepmother and instigator of the plot against him in the context of the manipulation, or was she already involved with it in the *Theseid*? It is necessary to concentrate first on the figure of Aigeus and to consider whether in the *Theseid* he was likely to have been presented as plotting against Theseus' life on his own initiative because of his fear of a popular young hero and potential contender for his throne, without the instigation of his wife.

It is suggested above that in the *Theseid* the theme under discussion was presented as the mythological prefiguration of the overthrow of the Peisistratids and the triumph of Kleisthenes. If this is correct, the figure of the stepmother was necessary, to represent the Peisistratids and to be a key figure in the table of correspondence between myth and historical events. But even if the hypothesis is incorrect, it is still unlikely that the stepmother was absent from the account of the plot in the *Theseid*.

First, if his wife were the instigator of the plot, Aigeus' guilt in attempting to murder a brave and popular young hero was considerably mitigated, his main defects becoming weakness and fear. And this was surely desirable in the context of the anti-Peisistratid propaganda which created the *Theseid*; otherwise Theseus, Kleisthenes' mythological prefiguration, would be presented as the heir of a tyrannical ruler. Second, it has been seen that in the *Theseid* the expedition against the bull was not part of the murder plot. The attempt against Theseus's life in the epic had involved only poison, as it does in sources which present the bull adventure as an independent deed (see, for instance, Plut. *Thes.* xii,2–3; Schol. A. *Il.* 741. Poison, as a treacherous weapon, would naturally be associated in Greek mentality with a woman, someone outside the political and social structure of the city (see n. 32 above), and not with an Athenian king. Third, no source has preserved a version in which Aigeus plotted against Theseus' life on his own initiative. If he had done so in the *Theseid*, we may have expected the variant to have survived, especially in view of the survival of the variant which presented the bull adventure as an independent deed. Finally, the inclusion of the figure of the stepmother benefits considerably the thematic pattern of the story. The requirements of the legend imposed that Aigeus should not be killed, and that Theseus should be aware of his father's identity, which meant that Aigeus could suffer no punishment for his hostility against his son. The inclusion of the figure of the stepmother allowed the negative elements of the "hostility of the parent" theme, including the punishment, to be focussed on her. It thus permitted the creation of an interesting thematic pattern which involved as far as desirable the father, in order to lead to the climax of the recognition of the erstwhile enemy as his son and heir. The stepmother, having initiated the hostility, attracted punishment, like Phaidra, and in a more complex way, Dirce and Sidero. I thus believe that the *Theseid* included the figure of the stepmother as the instigator of the murder plot against Theseus.

It is possible that in the late sixth century *Theseid* it was Aigeus who chased away his wife after the recognition; this is what happens in the variant of the myth given by Schol. A *Il.* 741; Eustath. Comm. on Dion. Per. 1017.20 and Myth. Vat. 48. In the light of the aims of the *Theseid* and the use it made of the "hostility of the parent" theme, it provides the most suitable context for this variant. In this epic Aigeus had the active and significant role at that point: whether or not my suggestion that he stood for the Athenian people is correct, it was he who performed the crucial act, the recognition of Theseus as his son and heir.[173] In the first half of the fifth century the theme was reinterpreted. As a result, the emphasis moved away from the motif of the recognition of Theseus by Aigeus, and hence also from the figure of Aigeus himself. This aspect was now taken for granted, and moreover, it had lost the primary political significance which it had had in the context of Kleisthenic propaganda. The emphasis shifted to the conflict between Theseus and Medea, and the defeat of Medea, which symbolised the conflict between Greece and Persia and the victory of the West and civilisation over the East and barbarism.

It is interesting to note that all sources which state the identity of the person who chased away Medea, only Apollod. *Epit.* i, 5–6 attributes the act to Theseus. It also presents the expedition against the bull as part of the murder plot. If I am correct in considering these variants as post-*Theseid*, Apollod. *Epit.* i, 5–6 appears to be based not on the *Theseid* but on a source which gave the version created in the first half of the fifth century.[174] I shall return to this point below. Medea is chased away by Aigeus in Schol. A *Il.* 741, and in the same account the murder plot involves only the attempted poisoning, as I suggest was the case in the *Theseid*. In other words, this source is following the late sixth century *Theseid*. The same is true of Eustath. Comm. on Dion. Per. 1017.20. Only Myth. Vat. 48 combines the variant of the bull adventure attributed to the first half of the fifth century with the motif of Aigeus chasing Medea. However, neither Schol. A *Il.* 741, nor Eustathius' commentary, nor indeed any other source, gives a wholly faithful account of the story narrated in the late sixth century *Theseid*. For, to return to the figure of the stepmother herself, the study by Professor Barron referred to in the Acknowledgments (p. vii) has convinced me that in the *Theseid* Aigeus had not been married to Medea, but to someone else.

The fact that no trace of the original stepmother has been preserved in the sources can easily be explained. Medea was mythologically a very strong and well-established figure who could easily overshadow an obscure one like Aigeus' wife, and Medea's claim to the role of Theseus' stepmother had the support of Sophocles and Euripides. The authority of these tragedians is surely likely to have had an overwhelming impact on the tradition with respect to the identity of the protagonists. Such elements as the nature of the expedition against the bull and the identity of the person who chased away Medea were less prone to be affected in the same way. And the ideological significance which came to be attached to the theme was inextricably bound with the person of Medea. This entails that, in the fifth century at least, Medea would have inextricably become bound with the story.

The hypothesis that the wicked stepmother had in the *Theseid* been someone else, replaced in the fifth century by Medea, makes good sense in the context of this development of the myth. If Medea had been Theseus' stepmother in the *Theseid*, the story would have involved Theseus, the Athenian hero, confronting and defeating Medea, the Oriental sorceress whose name lent itself to a direct association with the Persians: a myth of the last quarter of the sixth century would have contained by pure accident a motif which historical circumstances were to make significant about two decades later. I shall now consider how Medea came to replace Theseus' original stepmother.

The stepmother figure in the *Theseid* can be defined as follows. She is **female**, and thus outside the framework of the Greek *polis* as a political institution;[176] for this reason she exercises influence through **intrigue**. She tries to infringe Theseus' birthright and to cause his death: she is **against law and justice**[177] and an **attempted murderess**. Theseus is diametrically opposed to her. Not only is he **male**, and therefore belonging to the framework of the *polis*, but he is also a **king** and the author of the synoecism, the **founder of the Athenian state**; so he possesses **political wisdom**. He has shown **heroic valour**, and has **law and justice** on his side. After the Persian Wars, mythological themes which involved this type of binary opposition, between the "good" and the "bad", the "civilised" and the "uncivilised", lent themselves to an ideological reinterpretation and came to symbolise the Greek victories over Persia. The conflict between Theseus and his stepmother was particularly liable to this type of reinterpretation. For Theseus, the Athenian hero *par excellence*, was already seen as representing Athens, civilisation and culture. Moreover, he was believed actively to have helped the Athenians against the Persians at Marathon. In the context of this mythological activity, Medea's taking over the role of Theseus's stepmother and antagonist allowed the symbolism to become explicit. For Medea came from the East, and she also had a name which could be seen as related to that of the enemy and thus give rise to a story connecting Medea directly with that enemy — not to mention the fact that her maternal grandmother was called Perse.[178] It should be noted parenthetically that the story of the association between Medea and the Medes must have been invented at a time when the Greeks were particularly interested in the Medes and Persians, that is, in the years immediately after the Persian Wars. This association is always mentioned in the sources as resulting from Medea's expulsion from Attica after the failure of her plot against Theseus. There can, then, be little doubt that this tale was invented as part of the process of reinterpretation of the myth. In these circumstances, the takeover of the role also allowed the confrontation between Theseus and his stepmother, and Medea's defeat, to become the mythological prefiguration of the conflict between Greece and Persia. Medea could slide naturally into the role, replacing the obscure woman of the *Theseid*, because her character as already established in Greek legend corresponded perfectly: a dangerous, intriguing, unlawful female. The *persona* is the same, only the personality changed. Medea is however a polarised version of this *persona*: she is also a sorceress, possessing unusual, frightening powers, and a murderess. Whether she was said to have murdered her children before Euripides is not known, but she was certainly known at that time — on representational evidence — to have murdered Pelias.[179] As a result, in the new version, the binary opposition between Theseus and his antagonist became more polarised, and so did their confrontation. Polarisation frequently takes place within the mythopoeic process;[180] it is a main tool of "mythological grammar". In this case the polarisation was also positively desirable, reflecting well on the historical conflict of which the confrontation between Theseus and Medea was the mythological prefiguration. The more terrible and dangerous the enemy, the greater the glory of the glory of the victory; the more uncivilised and "wild", the greater the importance of his defeat.

Accepting these circumstances and that the way of looking at myth in the second quarter of the fifth century was coloured by the tendency to stress binary oppositions of the "civilised - uncivilised" type,[181] in order to use them for expressing the concept "Greek victories over Persia", Medea would naturally fill the role of the stepmother in the mythopoeic imagination of an author dealing in the years following the Persian Wars with the early career of Theseus.

Who was that author? Who introduced Medea into the story and generally reshaped the myth and reinterpreted it in an historical key? We have a *terminus ante quem* for Medea's participation, the early 470s, the date of the scenes of Makron and Myson. It appears to me that the woman attacked by Theseus in those scenes cannot be the stepmother of the *Theseid*, but must be Medea. By the 470s the story of the plot against Theseus had been known for decades during which it had not been deemed worthy of iconographical representation. This fact does not in any way invalidate the anti-Peisistratid interpretation of the theme suggested above (I should note that, if this interpretation is correct, the overthrow of the tyrants would correspond to Aigeus' chasing away of his wife, and not to Theseus' attack on her). The real circumstances of the expulsion were hardly flattering to the Athenians, and it is unlikely that attention should be drawn to them through emphasis on a theme perceived as a mythological prefiguration of that expulsion, however embellished was the image of the events in the myth. It should be remembered that representational art of the type of Greek vase-painting isolates and highlights motifs and cannot present an articulated and structured whole. So it is that motifs depicted in the context of propaganda must be of the "black or white" type, clear, simple and with an unambiguous message. The promotion of the figure of Theseus as a great anti-Peisistratid hero transmitted the message *that* Kleisthenes brought about the expulsion of the tyrants, which was desirable. But the emphasis on the actual expulsion which would have been produced by highlighting its corresponding mythological motif would have, by association of ideas, stressed *how* this had happened, which was not desirable.

Given that the theme had not previously been depicted and that in the early 470s any interest in the expulsion of the Peisistratids was surely focussed on the figures of the Tyrannicides, it would be surprising if, without any added stimulus, at least two unrelated vase-painters had suddenly decided to represent Theseus attacking his stepmother. It is also significant that Makron and Myson chose to depict a scene very important in the context of the reinterpretation of the legend, but less important before that re-interpretation and which had previously attracted no vase-painter's attention.

If it is to be supposed that the two scenes were painted before the legend had been reinterpreted, a curious coincidence would have to be postulated. Finally, it must be remembered that in the 470s the legend of Theseus had attracted special attention in Athens, biased by Kimonian propaganda which promoted the glorification of Theseus.[182] The appearance of a new subject in those years is thus *a priori* likely to have been part of that promotion, intended to glorify Theseus in a way relevant to Kimonian propaganda. The motif of Theseus attacking his stepmother did not belong to this category before the reinterpretation.

It is much more likely that this sudden interest in the subject was stimulated by the reshaping of the legend which transformed it into the mythological prefiguration of the Persian Wars. After the transformation, the scene of Theseus attacking Medea had a double significance, both aspects of which were relevant to the ideological preoccupations of the time. First, it glorified Theseus, who had defeated the dangerous Oriental sorceress and thus prefigured the victory of his people over the enemy from the East, a victory to which he had himself contributed by providing help at Marathon; and this reminder of Marathon was significant for Kimonian propaganda which glorified that victory at the expense of the others. Second, the scene commemorated the victory over the Persians, presented as a victory of civilisation over barbarism.

That only two scenes showing this subject have survived from the 470s could pose a problem. Why did the subject not attract greater popularity at the time? Why did the boom in these scenes not begin until the 460s? It could be that this reshaping of the legend had taken place in a literary work written in a *genre* not likely to have made a widespread and profound impact on the popular imagination, and thus not likely to have inspired vase-painters to any large extent. The work to which I attribute the reshaping and reinterpretation of the myth meets this last condition: it is Pherekydes' *Historiai*.[183] The boom in the 460s may be attributed to the influence of a play which, I believe, presented the new version in dramatic terms, and stated explicitly its ideological significance and the fact that it was the mythological prefiguration of the Persian Wars: Sophocles' *Aigeus*.

The publication date of Pherekydes' *Historiai* is uncertain,[184] but there can be little doubt that it should be placed in the first quarter of the fifth century. Indeed, a date in the 470s is very likely, coinciding with a period of intense Kimonian political and propaganda activity, the latter very largely focussing on Theseus. And the *Historiai* would fit well in that context, since Pherekydes had been connected with Kimon and the Philaids in general, and had treated the legend of Theseus in detail.[185] Since he probably used the *Theseid*,[186] it is to be expected that he would have taken an interest in the story of the attempted murder of Theseus by his father and stepmother.

Pherekydes' alterations of the legend seem mainly to have been political and propagandising.[187] The introduction of Medea and the ideological reinterpretation of the myth which gave it a new significance in terms of Kimonian propaganda is precisely the kind of mythopoeic activity he might be expected to undertake. But let us now approach the problem from another angle. I have argued that the *Theseid*'s account of the myth differed from that of the reshaped legend in three respects: the *Theseid* did not involve Medea; it presented the bull adventure as an independent deed; and it had Aigeus chasing away his guilty wife. In all surviving accounts of the myth Medea has displaced completely the original stepmother. With regard to the two remaining motifs, only one source, Apollodorus' *Biblioteca*, contains both variants which were created in the context of the reshaping and reinterpretation of the legend in the first half of the fifth century. This source (Apollod. i. ix, 28) also contains the story of Medea's connection with the Medes. Thus in the three points on which Apollodorus' account of the myth may be tested, it reflects not the *Theseid* but the version that I have attributed to the manipulation of the myth for which I suggested Pherekydes was responsible. In fact, Pherekydes is one of the main sources of Apollodorus' *Biblioteca*, and perhaps the main one.[188] The author to whom I attributed the manipulation of the legend is one of the main sources of the only mythographical work that contains the version which, on the basis of independent argument, I assigned to that manipulation, confirming at least to some extent the validity of the analysis.

The sudden boom in the popularity of the scenes in the 460s testifies to a sudden new, and very widespread, interest in the subject of Theseus attacking Medea. It is reasonable to place the prototype in major art — if this ever existed — in the same period, and to consider that major work the result of the same wave of interest. It had not been created in the 470s, when the reshaped and reinterpreted legend had attracted the attention of few vase-painters. Therefore the most appropriate moment for its creation was that in which interest was again focussed on our subject, this time much more intensely; in other words, the 460s. It is likely that both this creation in major art, and the boom in the scenes on vases, were inspired by the same stimulus which produced this new and widespread wave of interest in the subject. It is unlikely that the creation of the prototype could have inflamed the popular imagination to the extent testified by the vases, unless that work had been very important, artistically or politically, in which case its complete absence from surviving literary sources is inexplicable. In any case, the creation of the major work, about a decade after the motif had acquired its new significance, is best explained as inspired by an outside stimulus which focussed attention on the subject. In the 460s, after Eurymedon, the years were ripe for the glorification of a motif exalting the Athenian contribution against Persia. It makes perfect sense that Kimonian propaganda should make use of it. The stimulus which inflamed popular imagination and inspired so many scenes on vases must have been in a genre with widespread impact. Tragedy is such a genre *par excellence*. A tragedy produced in the 460s, dealing with Theseus's early adventures, including the fight with the bull at Marathon, the recognition, and the expulsion of Medea from Attica by Theseus must then be sought. It should present the myth as the mythological prefiguration of the Greek, and especially the Athenian, victory over Persia, and should preferably be the work of an author known to be associated with Kimon and his artistic circle, since this use of the theme would benefit primarily Kimonian propaganda.

One literary work does fulfil these conditions — except that its date is not known. It is Sophocles' *Aigeus*,[189] which dealt, as Pearson has noted,[190] with precisely this topic; the surviving fragments suggest that its climax was the recognition.[191] If it is the literary creation that stimulated the boom in scenes of Theseus attacking Medea, the early date indicated by the evidence of the vases would fit thematically (and as a result probably also stylistically) with Sophocles' early "bombastic" (ὄγκος) style, that of the period in which he was closer to Aeschylus.[192]

This is how I imagine the end of Sophocles' *Aigeus,* in the place relevant to the mythological motif of Theseus attacking Medea. After the recognition and the discovery of the plot to murder him, Theseus takes out his sword to kill Medea. She starts to flee, Theseus pursues her, sword in hand, and is about to attack her when there is an outside intervention: I believe that somebody makes a speech which stops Theseus. It could have been Aigeus, but is much more likely to have been a deity:[193] Poseidon, if he appears because of his association with Theseus, the aggressor; or, less likely, Helios, if the god appears because of his association with Medea, the prospective victim. Alternatively, it could have been Athena, associated both with Theseus and with Athens, the city being glorified through the hero. Indeed, Athena is, I think, the most likely candidate. I would imagine this deity to say something on the following lines:

> "Stop Theseus, do not kill her, let her go. Let her leave Athens in shame now that all
> her murderous plans have failed and she is defeated. You Medea, will be banished from
> the land of Greece for ever; you will go back to East, whence you came — an ill-fated
> journey for you, and for the Hellas, which brought you to these Greek shores. You
> will go to the land of the barbarians now called Arians, who will be known as Medes
> after you, for they will make you their queen. And after many years, these barbarians,
> these Medes of yours, will attack Greece and march against Athens, and they will try
> to revenge your humiliation and enslave the people of Athens. But at the same place
> where you, wretched sorceress, set a trap for Theseus, to be killed by a dangerous
> beast, and he defeated the beast and came back victorious, at the same place, at
> Marathon, your barbarians will be defeated by the Athenians and turned shamefully
> back, with all their mighty army. And as you tried again to kill Theseus by treacherous
> poison, so will they try again and come against the people of Greece, and they will be
> defeated and driven out of Greece for ever, like you. As for you, Theseus, you will
> help your people in their struggle and share in their victory, and you will be honoured
> for this as a god."

The idea that a deity intervened to avert the killing of Medea and to predict her future settlement in the land of the Medes is not pure fantasy. Theopompos' fr. 17 K from the *Theseus* runs:

> ἴξει δὲ Μήδων γαῖαν ἔνθα καρδάμων
> πλείστων ποιεῖται καὶ πράσων ἀβυρτάκη.

Mayer[194] thought that this fragment parodied a passage of Euripides and that the person to whom these words were addressed was Medos. Herter[195] however argued convincingly that the person addressed must be Medea, not Medos, since it is she, as a sorceress, who belongs to the land where the spicy sauces are prepared. Herter also seems to attribute the scene parodied by Theopompos to Euripides' *Aigeus* — or, at least, he does not appear to question that attribution. In a recent reconstruction of that part of the Theseus legend,[196] he includes after the recognition of Theseus by Aigeus and the exposure of Medea, a conciliatory intervention of a god who uttered prophecies. He bases this on the Theopompos fragment, and does not refer that fragment to a particular tragedy — except obliquely by referring to his note in *TdA* (see n. 195 above), where he mentions Mayer's attribution and questions Mayer's hypothesis with regard to the identity of the person to whom the words were addressed, but not with regard to the authorship of the *Aigeus* which Theopompos parodied. The attribution of the parodied passage to Euripides' *Aigeus*, in preference to the *Aigeus* by Sophocles, without even a mention of the possibility of the latter attribution, is probably due to the fact that very little attention has been paid to the latter play, although Pearson has reconstructed the general lines of its plot. That too involved the recognition of Theseus after the bull adventure and the poison attempt, and therefore also Medea's exposure and expulsion.

Theopompos' fragment shows that a divine intervention mentioning Medea's future settlement in the land of the Medes had indeed taken place in a play dealing with events connected with Theseus' arrival in Athens. Mention of Medea's settlement in the land of the enemy on the lips of a prophecying *deus ex machina* fits perfectly only the context of the reshaped and reinterpreted legend.[197] In context such a divine speech had a specific and important significance: it made the symbolism explicit and presented the myth clearly as the mythological prefiguration of the Greek victory over Persia. Theopompos' fragment indicates that there had indeed been a play which included the new version of Theseus' conflict with his stepmother, presented explicitly as a prefiguration of the historical conflict between Greece and Persia. The hypothesis that the boom in Theseus and Medea scenes was due to the production of such a play gains considerable confirmation. The scenes can place the production of the play in the 460s, a date which gains some confirmation from the consideration that the ideological reinterpretation of the legend was relevant and significant to Kimonian propaganda in the 460s, and especially after Eurymedon. It could not have had such a relevance at a much later moment. The play reflected in the Theopompos fragment and which presented the reshaped and reinterpreted legend cannot then have been Euripides' *Aigeus*. But it could have been Sophocles' *Aigeus*, the date of which we do not know. For Sophocles first competed in 470, 469 or 468.[198]

I should add that the play in which the presentation of the historico-ideological reinterpretation of the legend was a primary aim, or at least a very important one, would fit the young Sophocles much better than it does Euripides. The latter undoubtedly probed deep into the characters of the protagonists, the weak, henpecked king (Eur. *Aig.* fr. 3N), the scheming woman, the adolescent who comes rather cockily after sundry displays of valour (see perhaps op.cit. fr. 5), to claim his birthright, only to find himself confronted with a wicked stepmother (op.cit. fr. 4) who must be neutralised. But the adolescent Theseus whose conflict with Medea prefigured the victory over Persia was different: he was the mythological projection of the triumphant people of Kimonian Athens.

As for the prototype in major art which may be reflected in the scenes in question, Professor Martin Robertson has suggested to me that it may have been a sculptural group dedicated on the occasion of the victory of the *Aigeus* — if the play won a prize about which we are ignorant. Professor Robertson himself has suggested[199] that the statue known as "Amelung's Goddess", which he identified as Europa, could have been dedicated on the occasion of the victory of Aeschylus' *Carians*. Recently[200] he also advanced the hypothesis that the group of Prokne and Itys found on the Acropolis, and probably made by Alkamenes, may also have been dedicated on the occasion of a victory in poetic or dramatic competition; he notes that we know of two tragedies called *Tereus*, by Sophocles produced in 427 and by Philocles produced in 426, and that both dates would suit perfectly well the style of the statue. Professor Boardman has made a similar suggestion;[201] that the sculptural group of Athena and Marsyas by Myron may have been set up on the occasion of the victory of Melanippides' dithyramb *Marsyas*.

If my tentative reconstruction of the final speech of the *Aigeus* is on the right lines, Sophocles would be presenting Medea herself as going to the land of the Medes to become its ruler and thus to give her name to the land and its people. This is the version found in Herodotus, Pausanias, Dionysios Periegetes and Eustathios. In Apollodoros, Diodoros and Hyginus it is Medea's son, Medos, who is said to have been the ruler and to have given his name to the land and its people.[202] The fact that the latter version is found in Apollodoros may mean that this was the version given by Pherekydes. This is in fact very likely, for it is reasonable that Pherekydes should have moulded his story of the direct connection between Medea and the Medes according to pre-existing schemes to make it appear more plausible and easily acceptable.[203] This effect was achieved by the creation of the figure of a son for Medea who was given a name derivative from hers and identical with the Greek version of the ethnic Medes in the nominative singular. This allows Medea's son to be presented as a kind of *Stammvater* of the Medes, on the analogy of figures like Hellen, Arkas and so on. When Sophocles was writing, the connection would already have been established. He would therefore have been able to make that connection even more direct by associating Medea herself with land of the Medes and its people. This would have allowed the mythological symbolism to become more immediate and striking. This is fitting for a tragedy, and especially so for a divine speech in which the mythological symbolism, presented in dramatic terms, was made explicit.

Abbreviations used in the text and not explained in the notes

Alfieri/Arias, *Spina*	N. Alfieri, P.E. Arias and M. Hirmer, *Spina* (Florence 1958)
Beazley Gifts	Ashmolean Museum, Department of Antiquities. *Select Exhibition of Sir John and Lady Beazley's Gifts to the Ashmolean Museum 1912–1966* (Oxford 1967)
Breitenstein	N. Breitenstein, *Catalogue of Terracottas, Cypriot, Greek, Etrusco-Italian and Roman* (Copenhagen 1941)
Brommer, *SchlFasan*	F. Brommer, *Antike Kleinkunst in Schloss Fasanerie, Adolphseck* (Marburg 1955)
Brommer, *Denkmälerlisten*	F. Brommer, *Denkmälerlisten zur griechischen Heldensage. ii. Theseus-Bellerophon-Achill* (Marburg 1974)
Cambitoglou/Trendall	A. Cambitoglou and A.D. Trendall, *Apulian Red-figured Vase-Painters of the Plain Style* (1961)
CB	L.D. Caskey and J.D. Beazley, *Attic Vase-paintings in the Museum of Fine Arts, Boston* (Oxford 1931–63)
Ghali-Kahil, *Enlèv.*	L. Ghali-Kahil, *Les enlèvements et le retour d'Hélène* (Paris 1955)
Harrison, *Agora* xi	E.B. Harrison, *The Athenian Agora* xi. *Archaic and Archaistic Sculpture* (Princeton 1965)
Lambrinoudakis	B. Lambrinoudakis, Μητροτραφής. Μελέτη περὶ γονυμοποιοῦ τρώσεως ἢ δεσμεύσεως τοῦ ποδὸς ἐν τῇ ἀρχαίᾳ Ἑλληνικῇ Μυθολογίᾳ (Athens 1971)
Leach, *L-S*	E. Leach, *Lévi-Strauss* (London 1970)
Lévi-Strauss, *SA*	C. Lévi-Strauss, *Structural Anthropology* (Paris 1958, Engl. transl. 1963, ed. used here: Penguin 1972)
Pearson	A.C. Pearson, *The Fragments of Sophocles* (Cambridge 1917)
Peredolskaya	A. Peredolskaya, *Krasnofigurnie atticheskie vazi v Ermitazhe, Katalog* (Leningrad 1967)
Pottier	E. Pottier, *Vases antiques du Louvre* (Paris 1897–1922)
Rohden/Winnefeld	H. von Rohden and H. Winnefeld, *Architektonische römische Tonreliefs der Kaiserzeit* (Berlin and Stuttgart 1911)

Séchan, *Tragédie*   L. Séchan, *Etudes sur la tragédie grecque dans ses rapports avec la céramique* (Paris 1926)

Tillyard   E.M.W. Tillyard, *The Hope Vases* (Cambridge 1923)

Tischbein   W. Tischbein, *Collection of Engravings from Ancient Vases now in the possession of Sir William Hamilton* (Naples 1791–5)

Webster/Trendall   A.D. Trendall and T.B.L. Webster, *Illustrations of Greek Drama* (London 1971)

Notes

1. E. Pfuhl, *Malerei und Zeichnung der Griechen* (Munich 1923) — hereafter Pfuhl, *MuZ* — fig. 445; C. Dugas and R. Flacelière, *Thesée: images et récits* (Paris 1958) pl. 10; Peredolskaya, pls. lvi; clxxiii.6.11.

2. It might be thought possible that once the iconographical pattern was established it could also have been used to represent a different, but related, subject, or rather the same action-theme with different protagonists. But this is unlikely; for in such a case we would expect some additional element to characterise the other subject, and especially its protagonists, as different from the subject and the protagonists of the established pattern. Semiology teaches that the emitter of a message is concerned with eliminating ambiguity, which is one main reason for failure in communication (see J. Martinet, *Clefs pour la sémiologie* [Paris 1973] 36, 37). The use of the same signifier (in this case, the same iconographical scheme) to denote different signified without any additional element to differentiate them would result in ambiguity and failure of communication.

    Another *a priori* possibility is that not all vase-painters intended to represent a specific mythological subject, but that some may have wanted merely to depict a generic scheme of "youth attacking woman with sword", or have used the iconographical pattern merely for its decorative value without any thematic reference. But again, that would be possible only in cases where the iconographical pattern did not achieve great popularity; otherwise, an iconographical pattern used for depicting a very popular subject would, in artist's and viewer's mind, inextricably be bound with that subject. Our theme did achieve great popularity, especially in one particular period. In semiological terminology, the scene had become a highly codified sign. Codification (see P. Guiraud, *Semiology* [Engl. transl. London 1975] 24–5) is agreement of a sign among the users: they recognise the relation between the signifier and the signified. The more precise the convention, and the more people accept it, the more the sign is codified. There are several reasons for thinking that the scene under discussion was highly codified. I have mentioned its popularity and the concentration of this popularity in time, which would have entailed widespread knowledge of the relationship between signifier and signified. The simplicity of the scene also suggests that it could easily be decoded and without additional explanatory signs. Finally, "extracts" of the scene were also painted. This suggests that the whole scene could be signified through just a part of it, through a metonymic relationship (see E. Leach, *Culture and Communication* [Cambridge 1976] 12, 14). This could be done, and understood unambiguously by the spectator, only if there was high codification.

3. Dugas/Flacelière 64.

4. On motivation see Guiraud, op.cit. 25–7.

5. Motivation does not exclude convention: see Guiraud 26.

6. On high and low codification see Guiraud 24–5.

7. G. Neumann, *Gesten und Gebärden in der Griechischen Kunst* (Berlin 1965) 70 and n. 263.

8. Op.cit. 64.

9. A few random examples: Priam on the cup Louvre G 152 by the Brygos Painter (ARV^2 369,1); Lycurgus' son on the hydria Cracow National Museum (ex Czartoryski) 1225 by an undertermined Mannerist (ARV^2 1121,17); and compare more examples in *AJA* 58 (1954) pls. 58,15; 59, 20)

10. Op.cit. 72. On supplication in general see J. Gould, *JHS* 93 (1973) 74–103.

11. One suspects, perhaps unfairly, that the "playing about" interpretation was inspired less by a close examination of the iconographical pattern than by the inscriptions: these tell us that the protagonists are Theseus and Aithra: they were mother and son and are not known to have quarrelled violently to the point of Theseus attacking his mother; therefore this is not a scene of attack, and a different interpretation must be sought. This clearly is no sound method for interpreting iconographical motifs and patterns.

12. It is significant that the two artists are related: the Brygos Painter influenced Makron. See E. Paribeni in *EAA* iv, 791.

13. Pfuhl, *MuZ* 468; also Neumann, op.cit. 70.

14. Neumann, op.cit. 70.

15. Plut. *Thes.* vi. 2–3.

16. Lekythos by the Sabouroff Painter, Stockholm G 1701 (*ARV*^{2} 844,145; O. Antonsson, *Antik Konst, En Konstbok från Nationalmuseum* [Stockholm 1958] 97–9).

17. If I am right in interpreting the Empedokles cup near the Pithos Painter in the National Museum in Athens (*ARV*^{2} 141,1) as showing Theseus lifting the rock (*JHS* 91 [1971] 94 ff.), we have another early (last decade of the sixth century) representation of Theseus in the rock episode not only unarmed but also without the petasos.

18. *Oreste et Alcméon. Etude sur la projection légendair du matricide en Grèce.* (Paris 1959).

19. Delcourt, op.cit. 55–65.

20. Delcourt has considered the historical development of the myth and the form it takes in the different authors: op.cit. 19–30; 92–5. For bibliography on the iconography of the myth see J. Henle, *Greek Myths. A Vase-painter's notebook* (Bloomington and London 1973) 222–3, to which should be added M. Davies, *BCH* 93 (1969) 214–60; ibid, *Opusc. Rom.* 9 (1973) 117–24.

21. For details and the history of the motif see Delcourt op.cit.

22. The fact that the Erinyes do not appear in Sophocles' *Elektra* surely does not mean that Sophocles was adopting a version of the myth in which the Furies did not pursue Orestes. It is much more plausible that he chose not to bring them in at the end of the play for reasons of dramatic, and thematic, effect.

    On pollution and purification see E.R. Dodds, *The Greeks and the Irrational* (Berkeley and Los Angeles 1951) 35–7; 44; P.H.J. Lloyd-Jones, *The Justice of Zeus* (Berkeley, Los Angeles and London 1971) 70–7. Also M. Douglas, *Purity and Danger. An Analysis of Concepts of Pollution and Taboo* (London 1966) passim; on Erinyes, Lloyd-Jones, op.cit. 75–6.

23. In Stesichorus (fr. 40 Page [= fr. 217]) Apollo gave Orestes his bow to chase away the Erinyes. In Aeschylus' *Oresteia,* of course, his help was not "magical" but of a different order.

24. The story, or part of it, is found in the following sources: Thuc. ii. 102.5; Asklepiades, *FGrH* 12F 29; Sophocles, *Epigonoi* or *Eriphyle* (compare Pearson, i, 129–39); Sophocles, *Alcmeon* (compare Pearson, i, 68–71); Ephoros *FGrH* 70F 96; Apollod. iii.6.2; iii.7.5; Diod. iv. 65–6; Pausan. viii, xxiv,8; Hygin. Fab. 73; Ovid, *Met.* ix. 407 ff. See also Theodektas, Snell *TGF* i, 72 F 2; Accius *Epigoni*; Antiphanes fr. 191 Kock (ll. 8–11); Aristotle, *Poet.* 1453b, quoting Astydamas.

    Of these, the last two sources give a totally different version – or rather versions, if Antiphanes' expression is not in fact telescoping the story – from all the others. And it cannot be doubted that this was a variant developed in the fourth century. Antiphanes says that Alcmeon killed his mother μανείς, while Astydamas represented him as killing her without having realized that she was his mother. Delcourt (op.cit. 48) takes this to mean either confusion about her identity or a disturbed mind at the moment of the matricide. In my opinion it must have been a case of ignorance of her identity, since Aristotle mentions Alcmeon's crime together with the patricide committed by Oidipous and by Telegonos. The murder of the parent who has not been recognised, we shall see, appears in *patricide* stories, and is not found referred to the mother before this fourth century variant of Alcmeon's matricide. So the theme of parent-child hostility was dynamic enough in the fourth century to generate new patterns and adaptations. The tendency is obviously moralizing, since the crime has become less morally reprehensible: matricide for which Alcmeon was no longer responsible, either because he was mad when he committed it or because he did not know that it was his mother he was murdering. This tendency suits well the attitudes and preoccupations of the fourth century.

25. There are two versions of how the betrayal happened: see Delcourt op.cit. 34, 35.

26. It is sometimes thought that there was a version in which Alcmeon first killed his mother and then took part in the Epigonoi expedition. But the only evidence for this is Asklepiades' mode of expression. However, as Jacoby notes (commentary on *FGrH* 12F 29 [= i, 489]), such a conclusion based on an abbreviated version of this type is doubtful. Pearson (i, 131) remarks that the Erinyes would have been unprecedentedly obliging if they had waited for the end of the expedition to manifest themselves. Consequently it is, I think, implausible that such a version ever existed, though this does not in any way affect my analysis.

27. The Erinyes are not explicitly mentioned in all versions, but surely their presence is to be inferred from the mention of *nosos, mania* and so on.

28. Some association of Alcmeon with Delphi is also implied in Achaeus' *Alcmeon Satyrikos*, Snell, *TGF* 20F 12–13.

29. Op.cit. (n. 24).

30. Delcourt (op.cit. 47) also considers this "danger to the son" theme secondary and derivative.

31. I have not imposed a Lévi-Straussian model on the myth; I have simply attempted to use his method, with modifications, as one of the tools that may throw further light on the myth.

32. The woman is outside the framework of the Greek *polis* as a political institution: see P. Vidal-Naquet in *Récherches sur les structures sociales dans l'antiquité* (Paris 1970) 64. On the Greek mentality about women, see the important work of S. Pembroke, *Journal of the Economic and Social History of the Orient* 8 (1965) 217–47; *JWCI* 30 (1967) 1–35; and *Annales, Economies, Sociétés, Civilisations* 5 (1970) 1240–1270.

33. See below.

34. In the *Oresteia* the mediator of the opposition male-female, who establishes the final superiority of the male, is Athena, who though herself female, was born of a male only, and took on male roles. From the point of view of the opposition male-female, especially in its cultural aspect, Athena is ambivalent, though she is definitely not androgynous. (Delcourt op.cit. 91) takes a partly, but not wholly, similar view of Athena's character and her role as mediator between male and female.

35. E.R. Dodds, *The Ancient Concept of Progress* (Oxford 1973) 59 (reprint of an article first published in *PCPS* n.s. 6 [1960] 19–31): "Orestes' crime can neither be simply condemned as a crime nor simply justified as a duty, for it is both".

36. See also Dodds, op.cit. 55.

37. Klytaimestra's behaviour is stated in terms of disloyalty to her husband's oikos in Aesch. *Choeph.* 991–3.

38. Op.cit. 59.

39. Dodds (*Gr. and Irr.* 46–7) attributed these family tensions — which he rightly detected not only in the myths, but also in other aspects of Greek life — to historical factors which brought about the relaxation of the family bond. He connected this with the importance of the fear of pollution in archaic society and with the concept of Zeus. Lloyd-Jones (*Just. Zeus* 71) refuted this view.

40. Passim.

41. Op.cit. 35–6.

42. See below.

43. Especially: Dodds in *ACP* (see n. 35); C.W. MacLeod, *Maia* 25 (1973) 267–92; K.J. Dover, *JHS* 77 (1957) 230–7; Lloyd-Jones, *Just. Zeus* 90–5. Also A.J. Podlecki, *The Political Background of Aeschylean Tragedy* (Ann Arbor 1966).

44. He has also interwoven other themes of family tensions, Thyestes and his children and Iphigeneia, so that the matricide is contained within a general framework of polarised — because mythological — family tensions, further intensified by the fact that political power is also involved, since the family concerned is a royal family.

45. Given the context of this study, it is not possible to examine here the related themes of the murder of the grandfather or of the father-in-law, which would take us too far afield. On this, see very briefly Delcourt, op.cit. 56–7.

46. It is, of course, equally valid to consider this theme (and the "indirect stepmatricide variants") from the point of view of the death of the son, and classify it as a type of infanticide. But my subject here is the harm that eventually comes to the parent as a result of his/her hostility towards his/her child.

47. The theme of infanticide (as opposed to the cases of Hippolytos and Meleager [see Delcourt 55–7], though related, does not belong here. First, it does not involve any form of explicit and conscious hostility of the parent towards the child; and, second, the children involved are small, so that they remain totally passive characters.

48. On this myth see below, under "patricide".

49. Hom. *Il.* ix. 529–99; Hes. *Eoeae* fr. 23a Merkelbach/West; *Minyas* fr. 5 Kinkel; Aesch. *Choeph.* 603–611; Bacchylides, *Epin.* V. 95–154 Snell; Pausan, x, xxxi,4; Apollod. i.viii.2–3; Diod. iv.34; also Pearson ii, 64–6.

50. In the *Eoeae* and the *Minyas* Meleager is killed by Apollo during a war between the Aetolians and the Kouretes. This war also occurs in many of the versions in which the death of Meleager is caused by his mother.

51. Only the variant involving Althaia's having caused Meleager's death concerns us here.

52. The circumstances and the reasons for this vary in the different versions.

53. Either by cursing him and asking the gods for his death, or by burning a brand with which Meleager's life was tied up.

54. On this myth and its sources, see W.S. Barrett, *Euripides Hippolytos* (Oxford 1964) 6–45.

55. There are, of course, many other themes running across them and interwoven with them and with each other, to create the overall pattern of the myth.

56. In his commentary on Sophocles' *Kreousa*, ii,24.

57. On the myth, its sources and its variants, see J.G. Frazer, *Pausanias's Description of Greece* (London 1898) ii, 75–6 and Pearson i, 46–8.

58. This part of the story had been treated by Sophocles in the *Aleadai*; he dealt with the averted matricide in Mysia in the *Mysoi* (Pearson i, 46–8; ii, 70–7).

59. Telephos had consulted it while looking for his parents. Pearson ii, 71, conjectures that in another version he may have sought the oracle's advice on how to expiate the blood guilt he had incurred by killing his uncles.

60. This happens only in those versions of the myth which involve the theme of averted matricide.

61. The "psychological" dimension of this theme is the same as that of matricide and indirect matricide.

An interesting pair of opposites which run through the themes of indirect matricide and averted matricide is noted by Lévi-Strauss (*SA* 214–6; Leach, *L-S* 64) with reference to the myth of Oidipous: undervaluation and overvaluation of kinship.

Undervaluation of kinship	Overvaluation of kinship	Normal relations
1. Meleager kills his uncles.		
Althaia kills Meleager	Althaia kills Meleager	
	Althaia kills herself	

Normal relations are not restored, all ends in disaster

2. Kreousa exposes Ion		
	(Xouthos consults the oracle about his childlessness?)	
	Xouthos intends to introduce his alleged bastard son into his oikos	
Kreousa attempts to kill Ion.		
Ion attempts to kill Kreousa.		Recognition: normal relations restored.

Undervaluation of kinship	Overvaluation of kinship	Normal relations
3. Auge exposes Telephos		
Telephos kills his uncles		
	(Telephos consults oracle about his parents?)	
	Incest manqué between Auge and Telephos	
Auge attempts to kill Telephos.		
Telephos attempts to kill Auge.		
		Recognition: normal relations restored.

It is interesting to note that the undervaluation of kinship inherent in these myths of family tensions (see below for patricide) is balanced by elements of overvaluation. The myths would seem to confirm that binary opposites is one way in which the mythological mentality operates (see also Leach, *L-S* 87–8).

62. The theme of patricide has been considered in detail by Delcourt in *Oedipe ou la légende du conquérant* (Paris 1944) 66–97.

    For the Oidipous myth see especially Sophocles, *Oed. Rex* (and *Oed. Colon.*); Hom. *Od.* xi, 271–80 (and *Il.* xxiii, 679–80); Pind. *Ol.* ii, 38–42. For the rest of the sources, see Delcourt, *Oedipe*, passim. For sources and bibliography see G. Binder, *Die Aussetzung des Königskindes Kyros und Romulus* (Meisenheim am Glan 1964) 142–3.

63. *Telegony*, abstract by Proclus in Kinkel, *Ep.Gr.Fr.* 57–8; Apollod. *Epit.* vii, 36, and see Pearson ii, 105–10 on Sophocles, *Akanthoplex* or *Niptra*, with discussion of the myth; Hyg. *Fab.* 127. The full documentation of this myth can be found in A. Hartmann, *Untersuchungen über die Sagen vom Tod des Odysseus* (Munich 1917).

    It is interesting to note that Sophocles also dramatised the story of Odysseus' other son, Euryalos, killed by his father in ignorance of his identity, Pearson, i, 145–6. The hostility of father to son is here polarised in a way that makes the disaster stop at the son; it does not rebound on the father in a way that will cause his death. However, killing one's own son in ignorance of his identity is clearly disaster enough.

64. Apollod. iii, ii.1; Diod. v. 59, 1–4.

65. Dodds, *Gr. and Irr.* 36 implies that in the Homeric poems, Oidipous did not suffer the disaster which later Greeks associated with this sort of pollution; he infers it from the fact that in *Il.* 23, 679–80, we are told that Oidipous fell in battle and had an official burial. However, *Od.* 11, 271–80 tells us that the gods revealed the patricide and incest and Oidipous continued to rule in Thebes ἄλγεα πάσχων, while his mother, here called Epikaste, hanged herself, but left woes for Oidipous, ὅσσα τε μητρὸς Ἐρινύες ἐκτελέουσιν. It is clear that the precise form of the disasters which befell him may have differed in the earlier myth from later accounts, but there can be no doubt that he was even then believed to have suffered considerable disasters.

66. This is mentioned only in some versions. I should note that in the myth of Telegonos and Odysseus some of the hostility from father to son is absorbed by Telemachos: Odysseus sent him away from Ithaca in a vain attempt to prevent the fulfilment of the oracle, which he had associated with Telemachos.

67. The behaviour which Diodorus attributes to Althaimenes after the patricide – shunning human society and wandering alone in deserted places – is surely a version rationalised in a psychological key of the ritually imposed behaviour pattern of one tainted by pollution: not associating with others to avoid polluting them, placed "outside" the *polis* and society. This indicates that the myth has suffered much later manipulation by the mythographers.

68. In the notion of "original pattern" I am including all versions formed while the mentality which operated on the creation of the myth was still alive and operative, so that the myth was understood and reshaped in its own terms. When this is no longer the case, the myth is perceived by means of an external, moralistic or whatever set of values which distorts its earlier values and generates "corruption", as in the pollution motif in Diodorus. Lévi-Strauss' belief that all versions are equally important and should be studied together is valid only when the sole aim of the mythological study is to recover the mythological grammar on the basis of which the mythological material is shaped and arranged (through binary opposites, polarisations and so on). It can also be valid in an historical study which attempts to elucidate how different societies perceived and approached a given theme, provided the study is conducted historically and not in the historical vacuum advocated by Lévi-Strauss. It is not valid in the

study of the structure and significance of a particular myth in a specific historical and cultural context. And it is precisely this that is attempted here: the consideration of the themes of matricide, patricide, averted and indirect matricide in archaic and fifth-century Greece.

The mentality which would have exercised moral censorship, thus causing the corruption I am postulating, would be the same as that which created the two fourth-century versions of the myth of Alcmeon considered in n. 24.

69. Telegonos' transfer to the Isles of the Blest is, of course, a version of heroization.

70. This is valid only for male children since, according to Greek mentality, it is they who were significant and important social units.

It should be noted that the case of Paris is no exception. Although his exposure did not lead to patricide, there can be no doubt that Paris brought terrible disasters on his family and country, which led ultimately to the death of his father. The story of Tennes, which survives only in later mythographical sources, involves, like that of Theseus, the motif of the "dubious paternity": Tennes is sometimes said to be the son of Apollo, sometimes that of Kyknos, the man who banished him under the influence of false accusations. However, I think that the story of Tennes' death at the hands of Achilles indicates that in this case one paternity, that of Apollo, was primary. The story of Kyknos' paternity is likely to have arisen under the combined influence of the following two models: first, the motif of the "dubious paternity" which, as I shall argue below, was attached to several myths under the influence of the legends of Herakles and Theseus, the two major Greek heroes; and second, the motif of the father abandoning, banishing, or quarrelling with his son. At least one version of the Tennes myth includes an act of definite hostility against the father (Konon *FGrH* 26F 1 [xxviii]; Pausan. x. xiv,1–4). It is impossible to gather from the extant narrative whether or not this act had endangered the father's life.

For the story of Tennes, see Apollod. *Epit.* iii. 24–6; Pausan. x. xiv, 1–4; Konon *FGrH* 26 F 1 (xxviii); Tzetzes, Schol. Lycophr. *Alex* 232; Diod. V, 83; Steph. Byz. s.v. *Tenedos*; Plut. *Quaest. Graec.* xxviii (297 E–F); Suda s.v. *Tenedios anthropos.* Also Binder, op.cit. 138–9.

The strife between Phoenix and his father (Hom. *Il.* ix, 447–80) does not belong here: it did not involve abandonment or banishment of the son or any form of misuse of paternal authority or dereliction of paternal duty.

It is interesting to note that we have a case, that of the sons of Temenos (Apollod. ii.viii,5; Pausan. ii.xix.1), in which the sons do not themselves kill the father but hire a killer to do the job. Here too the hostility had originated with the father, who had deprived his sons of their rights.

71. A.R.W. Harrison, *The Law of Athens,* i. *The Family and Property* (Oxford 1968) 70–1.

72. Harrison, op.cit. 71.

73. Op.cit. 73.

74. Op.cit. 75.

75. This has already been noted by Leach (*L-S* 80).

76. In the sense defined above.

77. In some stories, the motif of the oracle is necessary, in the sense that it provides the reason for the hostility to the child which triggers the series of events. It is characteristic of the Greek mythological mentality that it was also imported in stories where it has no such role to play, as in the myth of Odysseus and Telegonos.

78. The opposition "overvaluation of kinship - undervaluation of kinship" noted by Lévi-Strauss (*SA* 214–6; see Leach, *L-S* 64) in the myth of Oidipous runs through the theme of patricide in general. The incest is an instance of overvaluation, while the abandonment of Oidipous as a baby and the patricide are cases of undervaluation. In the story of Telegonos, his abandonment by Odysseus, Odysseus' suspicions of Telemachos and the patricide are instances of undervaluation, matched by a censored overvaluation: not incest proper, but the marriage of Telegonos to his father's wife and his half-brother's mother. One version adds that Telemachos married Circe, his father's mistress and his half-brother's mother. In the myth of Althaimenes, as it stands, the undervaluation of the patricide (and in one version also of Althaimenes' murder of his sister) corresponds to the overvaluation which led Katreus to seek Althaimenes to bring him back to Crete; and also to the fact that Althaimenes' realisation of the patricide led to his death. In patricide, as in indirect matricide, normal relations are not restored, and catastrophe follows.

79. Pearson, i, 185–97. Also Hygin. *Fab.* 87, 88.

80. Here too, the undervaluation of kinship, involved in the aggression of Aigisthos against Thyestes, corresponds to the overvaluation involved in the incest between Thyestes and Pelopeia, itself an act of aggression. Normal relations are restored between father and son through the recognition, but not for Pelopeia who dies.

    It is interesting to note that in the story summarised in Hygin. *Fab.* 86, which (Pearson i, 187) was probably based on Euripides' *Pleisthenes* (for which see *TGF* pp. 556–8 N²), the roles of Thyestes and Atreus are reversed. There it is Thyestes who brings up as his own Atreus' son, Pleisthenes, and sends him to kill Atreus. In both stories the hostile relationship between father and son is polarised, as well as partly explained, by a corresponding and contrasting friendly relationship between the son and the father's enemy, who also happens to be the father's brother. In the story of Pleisthenes the outcome is different. Atreus kills his son under the impression that he was Thyestes' son. The structure of the latter part of the plot clearly resembles that of the story of Odysseus and Euryalos (see n. 63).

81. Delcourt 62–4 has classified this theme wrongly. For the myth of Tyro, Pelias, Neleus and Sidero and its sources, see Pearson, ii, 270–90. The main extant source for our motif is Apollod. i. 9,8. See also *Anth.Pal.*, iii, 9. For the myth of Antiope and its sources, Roscher i, 380–2.

82. Op.cit. 65.

83. The aspect of the Oidipous-Sphinx myth which is so interpreted by Delcourt (op.cit. 65), is seen by Lévi-Strauss as expressing the denial of the autochthonous origin of man (Lévi-Strauss, *SA* 214–6; also Leach, *L-S* 64–5). Since myths are multidimensional, both could be right.

84. There is a puzzling sentence in Hyginus (*Fab.* 246) according to which Aithra committed suicide "propter filiorum mortem". However, this unique story, which peculiarly attributes to Aithra more than one child, does not say that she was in any way responsible for the deaths of these children, and this is a necessary condition if the theme is to fall into the category of "indirect matricide". Nor indeed does Hyginus tell us whether Theseus was one of the children concerned. Such a story cannot easily be reconciled with the extant versions of Theseus' death.

85. Sources and discussion in H. Herter *RE* Suppl. 13 (1973) 1053–7.

86. A. Brelich, *Gli eroi greci. Un problema storico-religioso* (Rome 1958), 268–78; 305.

87. Leach, *CaC* 72.

88. Apollod., ii.iv,1. Also Brelich, op.cit. 297.

89. H. Herter, *RhMus* 85 (1936) 205–6; ib. *RE* Suppl. 13, 1503.

90. On this see also J.P. Barron, quoted above, p. vii.

91. J. Vancina, *Oral Tradition. A Study in Historical Methodology* (Engl. transl., Penguin ed., London 1973) 40–6; 76–113 and passim.

92. Vancina, op.cit. 62–4.

93. Vancina, op.cit. 63.

94. Pausan. ii, xxxiii.1.

95. It has been argued (recently by F. Will, *Korinthiaka* [Paris 1955] 196–7 with bibliography) that the connection of Poseidon with the root Aig- indicates that originally Aigeus had been a hypostasis of Poseidon. This theory has been refuted by Herter (*RE* Suppl. 13, 1054). I suggest that a false etymology may have been at the root of one paternity or the other. For example, it is conceivable that an epithet like Αἰγεΐδης, son of Aigeus, could have become isolated in oral tradition from the information that Theseus was the son of Aigeus, and reinterpreted (Vancina, op.cit. 44) as associating Theseus with Poseidon. Under the influence of the pull of Poseidon at Troezen, this could have resulted in making Theseus a son of Poseidon, on the model of the motif of the hero with one divine and one human parent.

96. On the Kalaureian Amphictyony, see R.M. Cook, *PCPS* 8 (1962) 21; J.N. Coldstream, *Greek Geometric Pottery. A Survey of Ten Local Styles and their Chronology* (London 1968) 337, 342–3; A.M. Snodgrass, *The Dark Age of Greece* (Edinburgh 1971) 402; N. Pharaklas, Τροιζηνία, Καλαύρεια, Μέθανα (Athens 1972) 20. Also T. Kelly, *AJA* 70 (1966) 113–21.

97. Bibliography in previous note. Kelly's arguments in favour of a seventh-century date I find totally unconvincing.

98. On this see V.R.d'A. Desborough, *The Greek Dark Ages* (London 1972) 158, 345–7; Coldstream, op.cit. 344.

99. On the rationalisation of the legend, see Herter, *RE* Suppl. 13, 1055.

100. The reason given may have been, as in the later myth, fear of the Pallantids. On this see J.P. Barron, quoted above, p. vii.

101. Also Brelich, *Eroi* 89.

102. On the theme of Aigeus' suicide, see also J.P. Barron, quoted above, p. vii.

103. The earliest date of the first appearance of the theme of averted matricide is uncertain. The earliest surviving evidence referring to a known "averted matricide" story is iconographical, and belongs to the first quarter of the fifth century: there are two representations of Telephos attacking his mother Auge on black-figured oinochoai of the Sèvres Class, Berlin 1937 (*ABV* 525,5) and Sèvres 2035 (*ABV* 525,6). They show a warrior attacking a woman, and a snake. The snake indicates the identities: Telephos attacked his mother Auge, and, but for a last-minute recognition, would have killed her because she tried to murder him. Beazley tentatively suggested that the two figures may be Alcmaeon and Eriphyle; however, the snake here is not associated with a tomb, as it can rarely be in the Alcmaeon and Eriphyle story, to indicate the connection of the matricide with Alcmaeon's dead father. On the two oinochoai the snake is "independent", the third participant in the scene; not a chthonic symbol but a figure which played a role in the story. This is made clear by its position in the syntax of the scene and by its size. There can thus be no doubt that the scene shows the averted matricide story involving Auge and Telephos, as suggested by O. Jahn (*AZ* 1853, 145–8). The *terminus ante quem* for the thematic pattern of averted matricide is the first quarter of the fifth century. I shall argue below that the story of the murder plot against Theseus was invented in the late sixth century *Theseid*. If the theme of averted matricide had then been extant, as were those of matricide, indirect matricide and patricide, the theme must have been created under the influence of the thematic pattern of averted matricide. This is indeed the most likely hypothesis. But if the averted matricide theme had not then been extant, we would have to suppose that the story of Theseus emerged from the theme of patricide, modified to meet the requirements of the story; and that this story had a determining influence on the creation of the thematic pattern of averted matricide, with which it shared the motif of the survival of the parent involved in the hostility.

    Similarly with the relationship between our theme and the story of Ion and Kreousa as told by Euripides: if the pattern of that story, which is, I shall argue below, closely related to that of our theme, was earlier than Euripides, and was already extant in the late sixth century, it would follow that the connection is due to the influence on our theme of the Ion-Kreousa story. If the pattern was a Euripidean invention, it must have been Euripides who modelled his pattern on that of the story of Theseus and his stepmother.

    I should add that it need by no means follow from the fact that the recognition motif, which is particularly suitable for tragedy, is the pivot of the theme of averted matricide, that this theme was first invented by a tragedian.

104. Pearson, i, 145–6.

105. J.P. Barron, quoted above, p. vii. Also, for a brief discussion with bibliography, *JHS* 91 (1971) 97–100.

106. *JHS* 91 (1971) 94–100.

107. For bibliography see the previous note. For a slightly different view, see J.P. Barron, quoted above, p. vii.

108. The fact that the stepmother is, like the tyrants, chased away rather than killed, indicates, I think, that the epic had been written after the overthrow of the Peisistratids.

109. For the earliest representation, N. Weill, *BCH* 83 (1959) 430–49. Also Herter, *RE* Suppl. 13, 1106.

110. P. Jacobstahl, *Theseus auf dem Meeresgrunde. Ein Beitrag zur Geschichte der griechischen Malerei* (Leipzig 1911) 6 On the motif see also Herter, op.cit. 1105–9.

111. H.R.W. Smith, *Der Lewismaler* (Leipzig 1939) 24.

112. V.A. Fromkin, *Scientific American* December 1973, 110–7.

113. Op.cit. 111 and passim.

114. Op.cit. 117.

115. On "noise" or "interference" see Martinet op.cit. (see n. 2) 32–4, 36–7.

116. I am considering the mechanics of the error to make clear that this kind of mistake in word selection is very plausible. By offering models about *how* this error could have happened, I am trying to strengthen my case *that* it happened.

117. Op.cit. 117.

118. The fact that only two words, the two names, were written on the tondo does not invalidate this: these two words were semiologically much less important than the iconographical elements, and therefore attention would not have been focussed on them.

119. For the arrival of Theseus and Theseus standing in front of Aigeus, see F. Brommer *Vasenlisten zur griechischen Heldensage*[3] (Marburg 1973) 213. On the iconography of Aigeus, ibid. in *Charites* (Festschrift Langlotz, Bonn 1957) 159–60. Theseus in these scenes is shown as a youth wearing a cloak, sandals, petasos, sword, spears. Aigeus is shown as a bearded old man with a sceptre.

120. A very tentative suggestion has been put forward in a negative way, that a cup by Douris could show Theseus chasing Medea: Herter (*RE* Suppl. 13, 1083) says, with regard to this episode: "ganz unsicher *ARV* 428,16". The cup is Cabinet des Médailles 538 (*ARV*^{2} 428,16), and includes, on A, an unexplained scene which can have no relation to the Theseus-Medea-Aigeus story: a youth and a girl face each other, drawn swords in hand, restrained by their companions.

121. Op.cit. 81.

122. I do not think that the amphora London E 264 by the Oinanthe Painter (*ARV*^{2} 579,1; *CVA* pl. 71a) shows Theseus' recognition. It may be showing "synoptically" Theseus' parentage: Aigeus, his human father, Poseidon, his divine father, and Aithra, his mother. If the scene showed an "episodic" recognition, Aithra would not be present but Medea would have been shown. But the woman in this scene cannot be Medea: she is making an affectionate gesture towards Theseus. Alternatively, the scene could depict Theseus leaving Troezen: the hand-clasp can be used in Greek iconography to indicate leave-taking, as well as "Verbindung". The old man would then be Theseus' grandfather, Pittheus. This interpretation, which is also accepted by Dugas and Flacelière, (op.cit. 85), would balance the subject of the obverse with that of the reverse, which shows a youth leaving home.

123. Brommer, *CVA* op.cit.; Webster/Trendall, op.cit.

124. On Bactrian bowls, see K.V. Trever, *Monuments of Graeco-Bactrian Art* (in Russian) (Moscow-Leningrad 1940); K. Weitzman, *The Art Bulletin* 25 (1943) 289–324. Also P. Denwood, *Iran* 11 (1973) 121–7.

125. Bibliography in Denwood op.cit.

126. Op.cit.

127. Op.cit.

128. Op.cit. 309.

129. In my opinion, Theseus in this scene recalls quite strongly the figure of Theseus in the scenes just preceding the recognition on the terracotta reliefs (above 3.I). But on the Bactrian bowl he is taking an active role, as opposed to his passive role on the reliefs in which Aigeus urges him to drink the poison.

130. *AJA* 60 (1956) 159–63; ib., *Hesperia* 31 (1962) 347–53. Also T.B.L. Webster, *AntClass* 34 (1965) 519–20; Webster/Trendall III.3.1; E. Simon in *EAA* iv, 954–5; T.B.L. Webster, *The Tragedies of Euripides* (London 1967) 77–9, 297–8. Add: neck-amphora in the Basle market in the group of Polygnotus (*MuM Basle Auktion* 34 [1967] no. 167, pl. 57). See also U. Hausmann, *Hellenistische Reliefbecher aus attischen und böotischen Werkstätten* (Stuttgart 1959) 69–94.

131. Op.cit. 161.

132. Guiraud, *Semiology* 29: "The ambiguity of the polysemic sign is in fact resolved by the content, and in a message the sign has in principle only one meaning."

133. Pausan. i.xv.3.

134. *EAA* iv, 954–5. The woman in Greek dress had also been identified as Medea by C. Robert, *Heldensage* 725.

135. Op.cit. 952.

136. And, of course, Medea preparing to kill her children in the Roman paintings is also wearing Greek dress.

137. Op.cit. 161 n. 16.

138. The two vases are the pelike Athens 13026 (N 1083) by the Painter of the Louvre Gigantomachy (ARV^2 1093,90); and a kalyx-krater at Agrigento by the Lugano Painter (ARV^2 1347).

139. Op.cit. 163.

140. Pearson i, 15.

141. *AntClass* op.cit. (n. 41).

142. D.L. Page ed., Euripides, *Medea* (Oxford 1952) lxii, n. 1.

143. Professor Martin Robertson has remarked to me that since the Mannerist hydriai generally have a many-figured scene round the shoulder, the scene on the Oxford fragment must be the left-hand end of a long composition. This does not affect the interpretation of the subject, but implies a different, and more complete, iconographical treatment of the episode.

144. It could be noted that the Geneva Painter belongs to the group of the Niobid Painter.

145. CB ii, 81.

146. Op.cit.

147. They are the following: Oinochoe Louvre G 439 by the Painter of the Brussels oinochoai – who, it should be remembered, also painted one of the "Theseus and Medea" scenes – (ARV^2 775,5); lekythos Erlangen 261 by the Nikon Painter (ARV^2 651,21); kalyx-krater New York 41.83 by the Persephone Painter (ARV^2 1012,3); kalyx-krater Bologna 298 by the Phiale Painter (ARV^2 1018,62) – Odysseus and Circe are surrounded by Odysseus' companions; bell-krater at Lancut, Potocki Collection (*CVA* Poland pl. 129,7; Brommer, *Vasenlisten*[3] 430,9) Pellegrini's drawing (G. Pellegrini, *Catalogo dei vasi greci delle necropoli felsinee* [Bologna 1912] of the kalyx-krater Bologna 298, in which the companions are also involved, does not show the skyphos, which is, however, clear in Stella's photograph (L.A. Stella, *Mitologia greca* [Turin 1956] 319).

148. This is also used once for Telephos and Auge: on the black-figure oinochoe Berlin 1937 of the Sèvres class (*ABV* 525,5; *AZ* 1853 pl. lx.1).

149. Ghali-Kahil, *Enlèv.* pls. xlix,1; 1; li,1; liii,1; lv.

150. It is impossible to establish the order in which the scheme was adopted for each of the three subjects. The present evidence would not contradict the hypothesis that the last subject to have adopted the scheme was Odysseus and Circe. If this were correct, we could understand why, among the two scenes involving mature pursuers, it was that of Odysseus and Circe which made use of additional elements to make its meaning clear, while Helen and Menelaos is differentiated negatively.

151. There is another scene, on the oinochoe Kassel T43 by the Shuvalov Painter (ARV^2 1206,1; *CVA* pl. 42.1–4), in which a youth wearing a pilos, cloak and sandals attacks a woman with a sword, left arm extended and holding the scabbard. Although the iconography of the young man resembles that of Theseus in our series, there are important differences: the woman is sitting on an altar, like the woman baring her breast in the "overt matricide" scene on the hydria Nauplia 180, of the group of Polygnotus (*ARV* 1061,154). Also, between her and the youth, Apollo is represented, indicating that the altar is an altar of Apollo. This fact, especially combined with the similarity with the "overt matricide" scene, which does not, however, extend to the baring of the breast, may indicate that, as Beazley tentatively suggests in ARV^2, the scene shows Ion's attack on Kreousa at Delphi. If, on the other hand, one wants to relate it to our series, it need not invalidate the Theseus-Medea interpretation. According to one source, (Plut. *Thes.* xii, 2–3), the attempted poisoning-recognition took place in the enclosure of Apollo Delphinios, where Aigeus once lived. The passage does not imply that there was already a sanctuary of Apollo there, but Pausan. x.xix.1 tells us that the temple of Apollo Delphinios was in the course of construction when Theseus arrived in Athens. The sources then could perhaps be taken as pointing to a connection, especially a topographical one, between the sanctuary of Apollo Delphinios and the events associated with Theseus' arrival in Athens.

   However, it is much more likely that the scene depicts Ion and Kreousa. The differences between it and our series surely make clear that the subject is not Theseus attacking Medea, the sign for which was highly codified, but the related averted matricide of Kreousa by Ion. The presence of Apollo would convey a Delphic setting, and probably also more specifically, the story of Ion and Kreousa in which Apollo was the third protagonist. Moreover, the fact that the woman is sitting on an altar relates this scene, at the iconographical level, with the representation of overt matricide mentioned above, with which the story of Ion and Kreousa is related at the thematic level, insofar as Kreousa was Ion's mother, while Medea was Theseus' stepmother.

152. M. Bieber, *The History of the Greek and Roman Theater* (Princeton 1961[2]) 148.

153. P. Arnott, *Greek Scenic Conventions in the Fifth Century B.C.* (Oxford 1962) 51–2.

154. It should be remembered that the enlarged version of the scene of the attempted poisoning — the event which immediately preceded, and caused, Theseus' attack on Medea — on the terracotta reliefs contains two such stock figures of female spectators — so they were not out of place in the story.

155. Something should perhaps be said about the scabbard. In some of our scenes the youth is holding the scabbard in his left hand, left arm extended (on no. 29 he is holding it in a different way, end outwards). This motif is by no means unique: it is found in a few scenes showing Menelaos' attack on Helen (see, for instance, Ghali-Kahil, *Enlèv.* pl. lv), and on some scenes with the quarrel of Ajax and Odysseus (see ARV^2 200,50), as well as on some earlier representations of Theseus, especially in the scene with the sow (see cup Villa Giulia 20760 by Skythes [ARV^2 83,14]). The motif of the left hand holding the scabbard with a himation thrown over the extended left arm also appears in the statue of Aristogeiton of the Tyrannicides group by Kritios and Nesiotes. A form of this stance had already been used for Theseus by Douris (on the cup London E 48, ARV^2 431,47), and the same artist used a similar stance for other figures (see cup Boston 00.338, ARV^2 427,4; very early work). Given this iconographical tradition, it would be, I think, unjustified to seek, as some scholars have done, an ideological significance in the use of the Tyrannicide stance for Theseus. On the other hand, it would be reasonable to believe that the Tyrannicide group of Kritios and Nesiotes rendered the stance popular. (On this type of stance, and on the use of the Harmodios stance for Theseus, see most recently E. Hudeczek, *ÖJh* 50 [1972–3] 134–49; also Ch. Kardara, *AJA* 55 [1951] 293–300; H. Thompson, *AJA* 66 [1962] 345–6). But the fact that the stance is not confined to Theseus even after the creation of the Tyrannicide group (see, for instance, cup Ferrara T.18 CVP by the Penthesilea Painter, ARV^2 882,35, side B), makes the hypothesis of the ideological significance unlikely. And it should, of course, be remembered that there is no evidence to suggest that the "founder of democracy/ liberator of the people" aspect of Theseus — which, according to the ideological hypothesis, would have been denoted through the iconographical assimilation to the Tyrannicides — was earlier than the fourth century.

   A further point should be noted. We have seen that in nos. 12 and 31 the stance of the left arm extended forwards holding the scabbard is different from that in other scenes; in nos. 12 and 31, the arm is bent at the elbow, so that the impression is given that the youth is "showing" the scabbard to the woman. The bent elbow is not, as far as I know, found elsewhere. In the rest of our scenes, and in others containing this stance-element, the left arm is unbent, whether or not a himation is thrown over it. We cannot know whether the modification was motivated by the desire to create the impression that the youth was showing the scabbard to the woman. I do not know whether anything can be made of the fact that both the Agrigento Painter and the Duomo Painter belong to the Mannerist school, but it cannot be excluded that the modification of the bent elbow may have been inspired by the subject. If it were so, that is if the impression that the youth is showing the scabbard to the woman was intentional, it would fit perfectly well in the framework of my interpretative hypothesis. The sword was one of the *gnorismata* left by Aigeus under the rock, through which he recognised Theseus as his son and thus averted the poisoning. It is in fact the sword that is always said by the sources to have attracted Aigeus' attention, and thus to have triggered the recognition. And of course in the concept of the sword the scabbard is included. In fact, in the Adolphseck krater with the recognition scene, Aigeus is examining the sword while it is still in its scabbard: he is seeing and recognising the scabbard and the handle. We cannot therefore exclude that these two scenes may have modified the motif of the striding figure, sword in right hand and scabbard in extended left, so as to use it for hinting at the reason for the attack. By making Theseus draw Medea's attention to the scabbard which authenticated him as Aigeus' son, the recognition motif which triggered the attack was included in the scene of the attack.

156. Professor Martin Robertson had kindly drawn my attention to another example of an adaptation of the iconography of erotic pursuit to denote an attack: Tereus attacking the fleeing Procne and Philomela, sword in hand, on an early classical column-krater at Agrigento (P. Griffo, *Il Museo civico di Agrigento* [Agrigento 1952] 28 fig. 7). Tereus is meant to be attacking both women, so in this case the iconography of the pursuit has been fully adapted and reinterpreted: both fleeing women are under attack. That the companion is not significant in our scenes is shown by the fact that she appears only four times, and only once, on Myson's scene, is she fleeing in the same direction as the woman under attack.

157. This table shows the distribution of the "scheme" and of its variants.
    1. Cup Leningrad 649 (St.830) by Makron: not scheme
    2. Oinochoe Boston 03.786 by Myson: scheme in non-crystallised form.
    3. Lekythos Oxford 1920.103 by the Providence Painter: scheme
    4. Astarita cup in Vatican by the Penthesilea Painter: scheme plus altar
    5. Pelike Manchester iii.1.41 by Hermonax: scheme
    6. Nolan amphora Cologne University Collection by Hermonax: scheme
    7. Hydria fr. Oxford 1966.508 by undetermined Mannerist: not scheme
    8. Stamnos London E 446 by the Painter of the Yale oinochoe: modified scheme— movement in different direction, grabbing by the hair, plus two spectators
    9. Bell-krater Leningrad 777 (St.1786) by the Painter of the Yale oinochoe: scheme
    10. Neck-amphora New York 41.162.155 by the Painter of the Yale oinochoe: scheme
    11. Cup Louvre C10932 by the Sabouroff Painter: modified scheme – movement from right to left
    12. Pelike at Charlcote, Fairfax-Lucy Collection by the Agrigento Painter: scheme
    13. Bell-krater Roman market by the Agrigento Painter: ?
    14. Volute krater fragment in Reggio by the Niobid Painter: uncertain – possibly scheme plus one or two spectators
    15. Hydria at Taranto by the Niobid Painter: apparently contaminated from the theme "youth with spears pursuing a woman"
    16. Hydria Louvre G 427 by the Geneva Painter: contaminated from the theme "youth with spears pursuing a woman"
    17. Stemless cup London E 128 by the Carlsruhe Painter: scheme
    18. Stemless cup once Deepdene, Hope T 177 by the Carlsruhe Painter: scheme
    19. Stemless cup at Warsaw by the Carlsruhe Painter: scheme
    20. Stemless cup Naples 2643 by the Carlsruhe Painter: scheme
    21. Stemless cup Arezzo 1428, 1430, 1434 frr. by the Carlsruhe Painter: ?
    22. Stemless cup, Italian market by the Carlsruhe Painter: ?
    23. Cup-skyphos Leningrad 1541 (St.1620) near the Carlsruhe Painter: scheme
    24. Oinochoe, Basle market by the Painter of the Brussels oinochoai: ?
    25. Skyphos Gotha 55 by a follower of Douris: scheme plus altar
    26. Skyphos in Mississipi by the Lewis Painter: modified scheme – the woman is not fleeing but facing the youth while making the usual gestures of supplication
    27. Skyphos Bologna 490 by the Painter of Louvre CA 1849: modified scheme – movement from right to left
    28. Neck-amphora in Naples, Museo di Capodimonte by an artist in the group of Polynotus: scheme contaminated – spear instead of sword
    29. Pelike Louvre C 10811 by the Painter of the Louvre Centauromachy: scheme plus companion
    30. Column-krater Paris market by the Naples Painter: scheme plus two spectators
    31. Column-krater Faenza I by the Duomo Painter: scheme
    32. Pelike Munich 2354 (J.243) recalls the Hasselmann Painter: scheme
    33. Cup Bologna 423 Submeidian group: modified scheme – grabbing by the hair plus altar.

        (Nolan amphora London E 333 by the Sabouroff Painter: scheme)

158. Martinet, op.cit. 118.

159. *JHS* 91 (1971) 108–9.

160. I know of no mention, in the literary evidence, of a Severe Style sculpture, or of a painting of the same period, representing Theseus attacking Medea. But this, obviously, cannot constitute an argument against the existence of such a prototype. Professor Martin Robertson kindly gave me a reference from Pliny (*N.H.* xxxv.137) where a Medea painting is mentioned in the proximity of one of Theseus. The passage refers to the fourth century painter Aristolaos, and it is not possible to decide whether the figures listed were isolated paintings, or whether they were combined to form groups (see Magi, *EAA* i,649). The passage reads: "Pausiae filius et discipulus Aristolaus e severissimis pictoribus fuit, cuius sunt Epaminondas, Pericles, Media, Virtus, Theseus, imago Atticae plebis, boum immolatio."

Leaving aside Medea, all the figures mentioned belong either to a political context or (once) to one of state religion, a fact which supports Pliny's assertion that Aristolaos was "e severissimis pictoribus". This makes it likely that Medea (if it is Medea that is meant here, and not, as Magi thinks possible (op.cit.), a personification of Persia) – was not shown by Aristolaos in the pictorially popular infanticide act, but in some other, more "severe" context. In fact, most political paintings mentioned by Pliny have an Athenian political association. So although it is only speculation that Aristolaos' Medea may have been painted together with Theseus, it is quite likely that she was shown in a political context associated with Athens. And, as I shall argue below, this is precisely the type of subject that I consider "Theseus attacking Medea" to be.

161. In a different thematic category from these extracts belong some white lekythoi by, and in the manner and by the workshop of, the Tymbos Painter – a painter of primarily funerary subjects. These lekythoi show a youth in the stance of our Theseus – indeed perhaps taken up from our scenes and extracts – charging in front of a tomb, or of a rock, this last with or without a snake. They are:

   1. New York 06.1021.127 (ARV^2 757,90) by the Tymbos Painter
   2. Koenigsberg 88 (ARV^2 759,91) by the Tymbos Painter
   3. Athens 1859 (ARV^2 758,92) by the Tymbos Painter
   4. Prague, National Museum 1675 (ARV^2 758,93) by the Tymbos Painter
   5. Louvre CA 2967 (ARV^2 760,37) by the workshop and in the manner of the Tymbos Painter
   6. Bologna PU 356 (ARV^2 760,38) by the workshop and in the manner of the Tymbos Painter

Here the extract has become decodified (see Guiraud, op.cit. 25) through its integration in a different iconographical context (tomb or rock) and its appearance on a different class of objects (funerary lekythoi, which at the end of the fifth century were decorated wtih subjects of funerary significance). It should be noted that this decodification takes place some time after the period of high concentration on the sign.

162. In whatever way one interprets the scene, and the other figures, the second man with the sceptre is problematic.

163. Leach, *CaC* 12;14.

164. In my opinion both personal and connected with the Alcmaeonid alliance (*JHS* 91 [1971] 109).

165. On representations of Theseus in free painting and their influence, see J.P. Barron, *JHS* 92 (1972) 20–45.

166. It is interesting to note in this context that the recognition of Theseus by Aigeus is never found in the surviving repertory of Attic vase-painting, from this or any other period.

167. R.W. Macan, *Herodotus. The seventh, eighth and ninth books.* vol. I.1 (London 1908), Commentary on Herodotus vii.62.

168. She takes part in the attempt herself, so it is a direct one. The corresponding feature in the historical events, almost certainly coincidental, could be found in the fact that the Persian king was himself leading the expedition.

169. I should note that my argument about the significance of the thematic motif of Theseus attacking Medea, and Medea's exile, does not depend on the acceptance of my interpretation of the iconographical motif and of the series of scenes considered in this paper. Even if I am wrong in thinking that the youth attacking a woman with a sword is Theseus attacking Medea, it remains true that in tragedy these events were said to have happened, and the symbolism referring to the Persian Wars could have operated whether or not the subject of Theseus attacking Medea was depicted on vases. Certainly the adventure of the Marathonian bull seen as a deadly trap set by Medea, which I consider as representing the victory at Marathon, had indeed found an iconographical expression.

170. On the glorification of Marathon at the expense of the other victories and on the "legend" of Marathon, see P. Amandry, *Theoria: Festschrift für W.-H. Schuchhardt* (Baden-Baden 1960) 1–8; N. Loraux, *REA* 75 (1973) 13–42.

171. See, for instance, Philochoros *FGrH* 328F 109 (= Plut. *Thes.* xiv). Also *testimonia* above pp. 22–24.

172. Amphora Cab.Méd. 174, by the Painter of Würzburg 252 (*ABV* 315,2); see Shefton, *Hesperia* 31 (1962) 347. Brommer (*Vasenlisten*[3] 252) seems doubtful about the identification of the subject. In my opinion, this scepticism is not justified, since we can exclude that the scene could show Heracles' struggle with the bull.

173. This need not exclude an attack on the stepmother by Theseus upon the discovery of the plot, which was stopped by Aigeus who decided to send his wife away from Attica.

174. On Apollod. *Bibl.*, see Van der Valk, *REG* 71 (1958) 100–68.

175. It is worth remembering that the names of two former wives of Aigeus, Meta and Chalciope, have survived. References in *RE* s.v. Aigeus.

176. See n. 32.

177. If my interpretation is right, she was also associated with the tyrants.

178. Already in Hom. *Od.* x, 137–9. Medea is also associated with two figures bearing the name "Perses": her father's brother and her grandson. These figures are attested only in later sources (references in *RE* s.v. "Perses"). Their invention was probably inspired by Medea's association with the Persian enemy established in the first half of the fifth century.

179. Also Pherekydes *FGrH* 3F 32, for an early testimony on her involvement in Apsyrtos' murder.

180. On polarisation in myth, see also Brelich, *Eroi greci* 277–8.

181. This is a more sophisticated version of Lévi-Strauss' basic binary opposition "nature-culture". This sophisticated version, because of its historical and ethnic significance, came to overlay the myths which contained the nature-culture opposition in its basic form, like the motif of the hero fighting a wild beast.

182. I have discussed this question elsewhere: *JHS* 91 (1971) 108–9.

183. It was Professor J.K. Davies who drew my attention to the importance of Pherekydes for the Theseus legend in the 470

184. Jacoby, *Mnemosyne* 13 (1947) 30–3; J.K. Davies, *Athenian Propertied Families* (Oxford 1971) 306 § xiii.

185. *FGrH* 3 F 148–153. On Pherekydes' connection with Kimon and the Philaidai, see Jacoby op.cit. and especially Davies op.cit.

186. Jacoby op.cit. 31 n. 46.

187. Davies op.cit. 306–7 on Oulios.

188. Van der Valk op.cit. 117; and 117–31; C. Robert, *De Apollodori Biblioteca* (Berlin 1873) 66–8. Robert believed that Apollodorus is not indebted to Pherekydes for his treatment of Attic myth. In my opinion this is incorrect; in the case of Theseus, Apollodoros' account of the adventure in Crete, and of the type of help Theseus received from Ariadne, appears to be indebted to Pherekydes (Apollod. *Epit.* i,7–9, and Pherekydes *FGrH* 3 F 148).

189. On Sophocles' connection with Kimon and especially with Kimon's artistic circle, see T.B.L. Webster, *An Introduction to Sophocles* (Oxford 1936) 8–10; William M. Calder III, *Philologus* 118 (1974) 213. It should be noted that Sophocles' connection with Kimon need not necessarily entail hostility to Pericles. On Sophocles' friendship with Herodotus, see Webster op.cit. 10–11.

190. Pearson, i,15.

191. Pearson, op.cit.

192. It is interesting to note that Sophocles appears to have been interested in myths of murder or averted murder of the parent. He dealt with matricide in the *Alcmeon,* the *Eriphyle* or *Epigonoi* and in the *Elektra,* averted matricide in the *Ion* and/or *Kreousa* and in the *Mysoi,* patricide in *Oidipous Rex* and *Odysseus Akanthoplex.* Moreover, he exploited a variation of the basic theme in the *Thyestes* which we have already considered. He also treated the story of Odysseus, Penelope and Euryalos, which is quite closely related to that of Aigeus, Medea and Theseus (Pearson i, 145–6).

193. I do not think that the fact that there is only one known case of Sophocles using a *deus ex machina* to turn the direction of the play and alter the expected outcome, in the *Philoctetes,* a late play, can argue against this hypothesis. (Athena in the *Ajax,* of course, does not perform this function: she is one more participant in the action). If I am correct, a *deus ex machina* would have been needed here, in the same way as in the *Philoctetes.* In both cases, the reason for the use of the device would have been the need to turn the plot in a direction different from that towards which it was led by the internal logic and dialectic of the play. In the *Aigeus* it was necessary that Medea should escape with her life and go to the land of the Medes. (On the use of the *deus ex machina* in Sophocles, see T.B.L. Webster, ed., Sophocles, *Philoctetes* [Cambridge 1970] commentary on v.1409).

194. M. Mayer, *De Euripidis mythopoeia* (Berlin 1883) 61f.

195. "Theseus der Athener" in *RhMus* 88 (1939) 318 n. 389 (hereafter *TdA*).

196. *RE* Suppl. 13, 1083.

197. Although we cannot exlude — but it is not very likely — that Euripides had repeated Sophocles' device and included a similar divine speech at the end of his *Aigeus.*

198. P.H.J. Lloyd-Jones, *AntClass* 33 (1964) 356.

199. *JWCI* 1957, 14.

200. *A History of Greek Art* (Cambridge 1975) 286–7.

201. *JHS* 76 (1956) 18–20.

202. *Testimonia* above. On Medos, see Roscher ii, cols. 2517–8.

203. Martinet, op.cit. 62.

PLATES

PLATE 1

a

b

PLATE 2

a

b

PLATE 3

a

b

PLATE 4